A CUCKOO IN THE NEST

A Play in Three Acts

BY

BEN TRAVERS

SAMUEL FRENCH LIMITED
LONDON

FOR AMATEUR PRODUCTION ENQUIRIES

UNITED KINGDOM AND WORLD EXCLUDING NORTH AMERICA

plays@SamuelFrench-London.co.uk

020 7255 4302/01

Each title is subject to availability from Samuel French, depending upon country of performance.

This play was first produced at the Aldwych Theatre, London, on July 22, 1925, with the following cast:

RAWLINS	Miss Ena Mason.
(maid at the Wykehams' flat)	
MRS. BONE . . .	Miss Grace Edwin.
MAJOR GEORGE BONE . .	Mr. Tom Walls.
BARBARA WYKEHAM . .	Miss Madge Saunders.
GLADYS	Miss Rene Vivian.
(maid at the " Stag and Hunt ")	
ALFRED	Mr. Roger Livesey.
(barman at the " Stag and Hunt ")	
MARGUERITE HICKETT .	Miss Yvonne Arnaud.
PETER WYKEHAM. . .	Mr. Ralph Lynn.
NOONY (a villager) . .	Mr. Gordon James.
MRS. SPOKER . . .	Miss Mary Brough.
(landlady of the " Stag and Hunt ")	
REV. CATHCART SLOLEY-JONES	Mr. J. Robertson Hare.
CLAUDE HICKETT, M.P. .	Mr. Hastings Lynn.
CHAUFFEUR . . .	Mr. Joe Grande.

ACT I

SCENE I. At the Wykehams' flat, Kensington. Tuesday evening.
SCENE 2. Parlour of the " Stag and Hunt " Inn, Maiden Blotton, Somerset. Tuesday night.

ACT II

Number Two Room of the " Stag and Hunt." Tuesday night.

ACT III

Parlour of the " Stag and Hunt." Wednesday morning.

A CUCKOO IN THE NEST

ACT I

SCENE 1

SCENE : *Sitting-room in the Wykehams' flat in Kensington.*
The curtain rises on an empty room in darkness. There is a
sustained ringing of an electric bell heard off.

> (*It is a small room not extensively furnished. What furni-*
> *ture there is is modern and new. A door* D. R. *Another*
> *door in back wall* C. *Window* L. *in alcove. A writing-*
> *table and telephone* L. *of door. Fireplace* R. *with club*
> *fender, easy chair* L. *of fireplace. A small bookcase with*
> *lamp on top* R. *of fireplace, a table with silver salver and*
> *telegram* D. R., *and chair* L. *of table. Settee* D. L. *and*
> *parallel with alcove. Pouffe cushion* D. L. *of settee and*
> *chair* D. L. *Standard lamp in front of alcove, stool* L. *of*
> *door up* C., *and close against writing-table. 'Phone book*
> *on top of writing-table and an A.B.C. time-table in*
> *pigeon-hole. Backcloth behind door when opened should*
> *suggest a fairly wide main passage leading from front*
> *door down the length of the flat*).

> (RAWLINS *crosses hastily from door* D. R., *which she closes,*
> *switches on lights* D. R. *and crosses to door* C., *which she*
> *leaves open. Her attitude suggests that she has been*
> *waiting for the bell and that it means something important.*
> MRS. BONE'S *voice can be heard off immediately after-*
> *wards.*)

MRS. BONE. (*Off.*) Is Mrs. Wykeham here ?
RAWLINS. (*Off.*) No, madam.
MRS. BONE. (*Off.*) No ?

> (MRS. BONE *enters. She is a tall and commanding lady of*
> *about forty-five with an overbearing manner. She comes*

*into the room quickly and suspiciously with a quick turn
of the head right and left.* RAWLINS *follows her.*)
Where is she then ? (*Crosses* D. R.)
RAWLINS. (*Up* R. C.) I don't know, madam. I had a tele-
gram to say she was coming back this evening. Alone, she
said ; but she hasn't come yet.
MRS. BONE. Coming back *alone* ?
RAWLINS. Yes, madam.
MRS. BONE. Where did she wire from ?
RAWLINS. Bristol, madam.
MRS. BONE. M'yes. (*As though to herself.*) I should like
to know what's happened.
RAWLINS. Yes, m'm ; but what have *you* heard, 'm ?
MRS. BONE. I and Major Bone—— (*Breaking off and turning
up* C. *in front of* RAWLINS.) Where is he ? (*Going to door* C. *and
calling.*) George ! George ! Come in, don't mooch about in
the passage.

(MRS. BONE D. R.   RAWLINS *crosses down* R. C. *just above*
L. *of* MRS. BONE.)
(MAJOR BONE *enters up* C.)
(MAJOR BONE *is a middle-aged man of military bearing,
rather a sporty type with an eye for a pretty girl and a
good judge of port.   He is in evening dress with overcoat
and opera hat.   He takes off opera hat as he enters.   He
comes down* L. C., *spots* RAWLINS ; *she is a pretty girl,
and he seems to be very interested, keeping his eyes on
her.*)

MRS. BONE. I and Major Bone had been out all day. When
we got home just now we found a telegram, also from Bristol.
(*To* BONE.) Where is it ? (*Crossing* C.) George !
MAJOR BONE. (*Pulling himself together.*) What ? Oh—yes.
(*Searching.*) All right.
MRS. BONE. Well, where is it ?
MAJOR BONE. (*Still searching.*) Half a minute.
MRS. BONE. (*Controlling herself in front of the servant.*)
Come along, do, something very serious has evidently happened.
MAJOR BONE. Yes, that's what you've been saying all along.

MRS. BONE. Well, where is the wire?
MAJOR BONE. (*After contortions.*) I know where it is all right. Don't be in such a hurry. (*Finds it in trousers pocket.*) Here you are—here it is. Don't snatch at the thing. You're always snatching at everything. (*Sits on settee down L.*)
MRS. BONE. (*Taking telegram from him.*) Now, listen. (*Reads to RAWLINS.*) " Be at my flat at seven, have had most startling and terrible experience, Barbara." That's what it says, and that's all we know. (*Pause. To RAWLINS.*) Do you know any more than that?
RAWLINS. (*After a moment's hesitation.*) W—well yes, 'm, in a way I do. (*Slight movement to MRS. BONE.*)
MRS. BONE. (*Looking at her closely.*) Yes—what? (*Slight pause.*) Come along now, you needn't be afraid. Does what you know concern my daughter's husband?
RAWLINS. Yes, 'm, it does.
MRS. BONE. I sensed it. (*Looks meaningly at MAJOR BONE. To RAWLINS.*) Go on!
RAWLINS. Well, madam, in the first place, Mr. and Mrs. Wykeham left here this afternoon for Paddington station as arranged.
MRS. BONE. Together?
RAWLINS. Yes, 'm. They were going to Somerset—to Lady Bunter's.
MRS. BONE. Yes, yes, *I* know. They left together for Paddington as arranged. Well?
RAWLINS. Some time later Mr. Wykeham came back here to the flat.
MRS. BONE. Alone?
RAWLINS. Well, without Mrs. Wykeham, 'm. But not alone. There was another person with him.
MRS. BONE. (*Warming to it.*) Who?
RAWLINS. I don't know who she was, 'm. A strange young lady, a foreigner it struck me—with a little dog.
MAJOR BONE. A little what?
RAWLINS. Dog.
MRS. BONE. Dog! Dog!
MAJOR BONE. Dog!

MRS. BONE. Go on!

RAWLINS. Mr. Wykeham didn't wait to explain anything to me. He seemed in a great hurry. He went straight to the telephone.

MRS. BONE. Were you here when he telephoned?

RAWLINS. Well—I was just outside the door, madam.

MRS. BONE. Yes? And who did he ring up?

RAWLINS. Gamble's Garridge, madam, for a car at once for a long journey.

MRS. BONE. (*To* MAJOR BONE, *with an intake of the breath.*) You see! (*To* RAWLINS.) Go on.

RAWLINS. They stayed here for some time. Then the hall porter rang up to say the car was below. And they went down together, 'm.

MRS. BONE. (*Nodding to her thoughts and speaking them aloud to* BONE.) I knew something of this sort would happen.

MAJOR BONE. (*To* RAWLINS.) What happened to the little dog?

RAWLINS. Oh, she took the dog with her, sir, thank goodness. It was here too long as it was.

MRS. BONE. (*Still ruminating.*) I sensed it. (*Sniff—pause.*) Can the hall porter throw any light?

RAWLINS. No 'm. He said there was luggage. That's all he knew.

MRS. BONE. Luggage? And Mr. Wykeham told you *nothing*? (C.)

RAWLINS. Well, of course, when I first saw him, madam, I said, " What, sir? Haven't you caught the train?" and he said: " Mrs. Wykeham caught it," he said, " and I reely caught it too, only I let it go again," he said.

MRS. BONE. And have you no idea where he and this person were bound for in the car?

RAWLINS. None whatever, madam.

MRS. BONE. Nor has the hall porter?

RAWLINS. No, 'm, oh—but there's another telegram here, 'm. (*Crosses to table* R.)

MRS. BONE. (*Keenly and quickly.*) Another? Where?

(RAWLINS *takes salver with telegram from table.* MRS. BONE *makes a move to take it.*)

RAWLINS. I didn't open it because it's addressed "Wykeham," but of course it may be from Mr. Wykeham to Mrs. Wykeham.

MRS. BONE. I'll take it.

(RAWLINS *hands it to her reluctantly.*) Very well, you needn't wait, Rawlins. I shall stay here until Mrs. Wykeham returns. (*Crosses to* C.)

RAWLINS. Thank you, 'm.

(MRS. BONE, C., *is reading telegram to herself as* MAJOR BONE *and* RAWLINS *exchange glances.* RAWLINS *smiles cheekily at him as she goes out* D. R.)

MRS. BONE. (*Reading, crosses* L.) " Returning immediately. Wait for me at home. Very put out. Barbara." Well, nobody can say that I am wise *after* the event.

MAJOR BONE. I'm afraid I'm not wise at all.

MRS. BONE. (*Crosses* L.) I know you're not.

MAJOR BONE. Thank you very much.

MRS. BONE. If you'd been wise, you'd have forbidden this marriage. I disliked the man from the very first. I told you so.

MAJOR BONE. You did.

MRS. BONE. (*Crosses* C.) A dark horse and a loose fish.

MAJOR BONE. But you've nothing to go on yet, you know.

MRS. BONE. (*Turning to him.*) Nothing to go on! He's *left* her. Don't tell me. A flash foreign woman with a little dog. (*Going* R.)

MAJOR BONE. (*Rising and crossing to* C.) Very likely Barbara knows all about it.

MRS. BONE. (*Wheeling on him again and flourishing her own telegram.*) This is what Barbara knows. (*Reads.*) " Most startling and terrible experience." (*Reads from the other telegram.*) " Returning immediately. Very put out." Oh, I don't suppose it's the first time since they've been married. I expect he's living with this woman.

MAJOR BONE. Oh, nonstence, Constance. (*He turns up stage.*)

MRS. BONE. (*Puts telegram on table* R. C. *Wheeling round on him as before.*) What do you mean? Here he is, in a car. With this woman.

MAJOR BONE. (*Suddenly inspired.*) By Jove! I have it! (L. C.) Don't you see?

MRS. BONE. What?

MAJOR BONE. (*Coming down.*) He missed the train, so he took a car and went after Barbara.

MRS. BONE. *After* Barbara? Oh, then why did he start by going *away* from Barbara?

MAJOR BONE. Oh, very likely he didn't on purpose.

MRS. BONE. Now what d'you mean? How can he be living with another woman but not on purpose?

MAJOR BONE. He isn't living with her, Constance, whatever it is. You can't call it that.

MRS. BONE. I prefer to call it that.

MAJOR BONE. But what evidence have you got? (*Sits* L. C.)

MRS. BONE. (*Pointedly.*) Evidence! He gives Barbara the slip and packs her off in an express train. Then he goes off in a car with luggage, on a long journey, with a woman. That was several hours ago, and there's no news of him. That's enough for me. I know what men are. (*Cross* L., *with emphasis.*) It's no good your telling me.

(MAJOR BONE *turns hopelessly away.*)

MAJOR BONE. (*Sitting.*) I know that. Well, we'll wait and see what *Barbara* has got to say.

MRS. BONE. (*Cross* R. C., *picks up wires, glances at them and replaces them on table, and cross again* L. C. *to* MAJOR.) Yes, and don't forget that you listened to Barbara from the first, and if you had listened to *me*——

(*Electric door-bell, off.*)

Thank goodness! Here she is. (*Up* C.)

MAJOR BONE. It may be him. (*Crosses to* MRS. BONE.)

MRS. BONE. (*With sarcasm.*) It *may* be, yes! You stop where you are—I'll let her in.

(*She goes out* C.)

(MAJOR BONE *heaves a very deep sigh and sits* L. *After a moment the voices of* MRS. BONE *and* BARBARA *are heard in the passage.*)

(*Off.*) My poor child!

BARBARA. (*Off.*) Oh, mother!

MRS. BONE. (*Off.*) Come in !

BARBARA. (*Off.*) Is Peter here ?

(BARBARA *enters. She is a handsome woman of thirty; she can be as biting as her mother but she has something of her father's gentler, yearning nature.*)

MRS. BONE. No, dear, he is not. (*Reappearing.*) It *is* Barbara. (C.)

MAJOR BONE. (*Plaintively.*) Yes, I guessed it would be.

BARBARA. Oh, so father's here, too. (*Crosses down* R.)

MAJOR BONE. Yes. Father's here all right.

MRS. BONE. Yes, I brought him. (*Crosses* R.)

MAJOR BONE. You did.

BARBARA. (*Coming down* R.) I've had a terrible time. Is Rawlins here ?

MRS. BONE. Yes. Never mind about Rawlins. (*Crosses* R. *to* BARBARA.)

BARBARA. But I left my luggage downstairs.

MRS. BONE. Never mind about that, dear. Tell me all. Tell me all.

BARBARA. (*Sits on seat* R. C.) I'm absolutely fagged out. Father, there's some wine in the dining-room sideboard. Go and get some, will you ?

MAJOR BONE. (*Rising promptly, cross up* C.) Oh, thank you very, very much, my dear. That's very kind of you.

BARBARA. For me, I mean. (*Rising, takes coat and hat off. Puts coat on club fender* R., *hat and gloves on bookcase.*)

MAJOR BONE. (*Pausing at door* C.) Oh, I see. (*Closes door.*) Well—er—where are the glasses ? (*Crosses* L. C.)

MRS. BONE. (*Swinging on him furiously.*) Oh, don't fiddle and diddle ! Get the wine !

(*He turns again to the door.*)

(*To* BARBARA.) Now, my poor child.

BARBARA. (*Sitting* R. C.) I hardly know how to start telling you what has happened. (*She pauses.*)

(MRS. BONE *at* BARBARA'S *side* R. MAJOR BONE *still hovers up* C. *listening.*)

MRS. BONE. (*Shortly and practically.*) Well, try, dear.

BARBARA. Peter and I went to Paddington. We got in the train, both of us. In an empty carriage, to ourselves, I mean——

(BONE *closes door* C. *quietly.*)

MRS. BONE. Yes? Yes? Yes?

(BONE *comes down* R. C.)

BARBARA. Peter got out and went to get some papers. I waited, and he came back, but he didn't get back into the carriage. He stood on the platform and fumbled and said the girl at the bookstall had given him the wrong change or something.

MRS. BONE. Huh!—mh!—huh!

(BONE *looks at* MRS. BONE.)

BARBARA. By this time they were shutting the doors and saying, " Take your seats, please." You know how they do.

MAJOR BONE. M'yes!

MRS. BONE. (*Turning her head.*) Get the wine!

MAJOR BONE. But I'd like to hear this. Do you mind if I just listen for a moment? I shall keep very quiet.

BARBARA. Before I could stop him, Peter went back to the bookstall. And the next thing I knew was the train began to move. You know how the big express trains glide out. I could scarcely realise it for a moment. So I jumped up and put my head through the window.

MAJOR BONE. Good God!

BARBARA. (*Severely to him.*) The window was open.

MAJOR BONE. Oh, I see.

BARBARA. There in the distance I saw Peter. He was standing with his back to the train talking to a young woman. She was no one *I* knew.

MRS. BONE. (*Quite complacently.*) And what did *you do*?

BARBARA. What *could* I do? I shouted to a porter who was apparently a deaf mute. I waved. No-one took the slightest notice, except one offensive looking man who waved back.

MRS. BONE. And—your husband?

BARBARA. Peter never so much as turned his head.

MRS. BONE. You should have rung the alarm bell.

MAJOR BONE. Oh, I don't suppose he'd have heard it!

MRS. BONE. (*Swinging round at him.*)   Will you get the wine ? The wine !

(BONE *nods his head.*)

MAJOR BONE. ⎫ (*To* BARBARA.)   Go on, dear.
MRS. BONE. ⎭

MAJOR BONE.   Oh, sorry !

BARBARA.   Well, there I was.   I tried to control myself and think.   I had all our luggage in the train, his and mine.

MRS. BONE.   Go on, dear.

BARBARA.   The first stop was Bristol.   I got out there.   I wasn't going to Peter's friends in the country with a story like that.   So I wired him and you and Rawlins and came back here. Now, mother, what does it all mean ?

MAJOR BONE. (*Advancing importantly.*)   Now you listen to me, my dear.   I'm a man of the world.   I'll soon put this right. Had the lady a little dog ?

MRS. BONE.   The *wine* !   The *wine* !

MAJOR BONE.   Yes, I heard you say that before.

BARBARA. (*Scornfully.*)   What lady ?

MAJOR BONE.   Peter's pal—gal, I mean !   Well, damn it— the woman person we're discussing.   I must call her something. Had she a little dog ?

BARBARA.   What difference does that make ?

MAJOR BONE.   Yes, but had she ?

BARBARA.   Yes, I remember she did have a beastly little dog.

MAJOR BONE. (*To* MRS. BONE.)   There you are, my dear, the plot thickens.

MRS. BONE.   George !

MAJOR BONE.   The wine !

MRS. BONE.   Yes !

MAJOR BONE.   Right !

(*He goes out hastily* C., *leaving door open.*)

BARBARA.   Mother, what does he mean ?   " The plot thickens " ? (*Rises, crosses* D. C.)

MRS. BONE.   Now, Barbara, let me tell *you.*   I have seen Rawlins.   Your husband came back to the flat here with a woman !

BARBARA. What? Who *is* she?

MRS. BONE. That remains to be seen. But he brought her here and rang up for a car.

BARBARA. A car? Oh, then, perhaps——

MRS. BONE. And took the woman and her luggage away with him in the car. We don't know where to. But a long way away. (*Sits* L.)

BARBARA. And he's not come back? (*Sits with* MRS. BONE.)

MRS. BONE. No. (*Cross to settee* L.)

BARBARA. (*Breaking down.*) Oh, mother!

MRS. BONE. There, there! You mustn't break down. No, no. (*Calling.*) George—hurry up with the wine!

MAJOR BONE. (*Off.*) All right, my dear; do you want the port or the hock? I can recommend the port.

MRS. BONE. The port. Hurry. (*To* BARBARA.) There, my dear. Don't give way. (*Caressing her.*) Of course, I always expected this, and said so.

(BONE *appears with wine* C.)

BARBARA. You think he missed the train on purpose?

MRS. BONE. To be quite candid, I think he missed it by appointment.

(*Enter* BONE.)

BARBARA. But why should he bring her back here?

MAJOR BONE. (*Crosses to table with port and glasses.*) There you are, that's what I say, that's a point in his favour. (*Places tray with wine on table.*)

MRS. BONE. (*Turning on him.*) Oh, you! Do something sensible. Ring up Gamble's Garage on the telephone.

MAJOR BONE. On the telephone? Why? What's the idea? I think he's with these people the Bunters by this time. I'll wire them and find out. (*Crosses up* C.)

MRS. BONE. Yes, (*rising*) and lug it into the public eye. No, thank you.

MAJOR BONE. Well, naturally, I mean to say, a judiciously worded wire. (*Turning over leaves of telephone directory, which he has taken from table up* L.) You know, sort of—" Wykeham

missed train, wife caught ; he wouldn't come, so she didn't go,"
or words to that effect.

MRS. BONE.   Oh, stop !   (*Crosses up* R. *behind settee.*) Fiddling
and fuddling !   Have you got that number ?

MAJOR BONE.   Yes, here it is.   What shall I do with it ?

MRS. BONE.   Ask for it.

MAJOR BONE.   Ask for it ?   Right.   (*Closes book and replaces
it on table up* L.)   Ask for the number, eh ?   What is the damned
number ?

(MRS. BONE *tries to get 'phone book.*)

BARBARA.   Oh, father !   (*Rises from settee.*)

MAJOR BONE.   (*Sits at 'phone table.*)   All right—all right—
I've got it.   Ah—ah—Kensington 1040.   (*Closes book.*)

MRS. BONE.   I'll speak.

MAJOR BONE.   Oh !   That'll be a very nice change.   (*Looks at*
BARBARA *knowingly.*)   But just for once in a way you let me have
a say.   I think we should wire, we ought to enquire——

MRS. BONE.   Are you trying to be funny ?

MAJOR BONE.   (*On 'phone.*)   Oh, Lord !   There you are,
you see, the same old story, when father suggests anything—
what ?—Yes, I'm here.   Is that whatever the number is ?   Are
you Thingamebob's Whatsaname ?   What is it ?

BARBARA.   The garage.

MAJOR BONE.   (*Stamps foot impatiently.*)   The garage.

MRS. BONE.   (*Taking 'phone from him.*)   Give it to me—give
it to me.

(BONE *crosses* R. C. *and looks appealingly at* BARBARA.
BARBARA *intently listening.*)

Are you Gamble's Garage ?   I am speaking for Mrs. Wykeham.
Mr. Wykeham engaged a car to-day.   Where for ?   Do you
know ?

MAJOR BONE.   The maid said that when they came—— (C.)

MRS. BONE.   (*To* BONE.)   Quiet !   You do ?   What ?   Oh,
you've just heard.   Where ?   Where ?   What ?

MAJOR BONE.   What's he say ?

BARBARA.   What, mother ?   (*Rising.*)

MRS. BONE. Hush, darling! (*On 'phone.*) Where, though? To *what* place? Maidens-*what*?

MAJOR BONE. What's that?

MRS. BONE. (*To* BONE.) George! (*On 'phone.*) Blot? Blotton. Oh, Blotton. Where is that? Oh! Oh! Yes? Yes? Thank you. Yes. Yes. Thank you. Very well. (*Rings off.*)

(BONE *crosses to table* R. *and helps himself to port.*)

BARBARA. What, mother? Quickly!

(BARBARA *comes down* L. *of settee towards* C.)

MRS. BONE. (*Deliberately.*) The garage has just heard the car broke down on a lonely road. They went off together to find the nearest hotel. The chauffeur got a lift on a motor cycle and telephoned to Gamble's.

BARBARA. Where is the place where Peter's gone?

MRS. BONE. They set out to walk to a place called Maiden Blotton.

BARBARA. Where's that?

MRS. BONE. They think Somerset. But——

MAJOR BONE. (*Rising, triumphantly.*) Somerset! There you are! I told you so! He's gone after Barbara.

BARBARA. What?

MAJOR BONE. Of course. It stands to reason. You had all his things.

MRS. BONE. Things?

MAJOR BONE. Yes.

MRS. BONE. What things?

MAJOR BONE. Ah, clothes and things.

MRS. BONE. What things?

MAJOR BONE. Oh, Lord, clothes and things, don't you see? He went after Barbara. He thinks she's at the Buntings.

MRS. BONE. Then why didn't he go on to the Bunters?

MAJOR BONE. Well, very likely he did.

MRS. BONE. With a woman?

MAJOR BONE. Well, I can't be supposed to know everything. I'm not a clairvoyant.

MRS. BONE. Oh, be quiet!

BARBARA. I shall go down to this hotel. (*Crosses up stage.*)

(BONE *is about to have another drink.*)

MRS. BONE. Yes, first thing to-morrow. (*She sees* BONE *with the decanter, crosses to* R. *above table.*)

BARBARA. I can go to-night.

MRS. BONE. (*Takes wine from* BONE, *who is about to drink.*) Oh, no, you don't, you've had quite enough of that !

BARBARA. (*To* BONE.) I can get a train to Bristol and motor on from there.

MRS. BONE. (*Replaces wine decanter on table and crosses* C. *to* BARBARA.) Not to-night, dear.

(BARBARA *has gone to writing-table and got an A.B.C.*)

BARBARA. (*Looking up train.*) If I wait till to-morrow and there's anything wrong—it might be too late. Look, Paddington, 8 o'clock. Arrive Bristol 10.20.

MRS. BONE. Yes, and then you'll have to motor out to this place.

MAJOR BONE. 'M, yes. I should think you'd be too late even if you did go to-night.

MRS. BONE. Oh, you seem very experienced !

MAJOR BONE. No—just an ordinary public school education.

MRS. BONE. (*To* BARBARA.) Do what I advise, dear. What is the first train to-morrow ?

BARBARA. 5.30 A.M. Bristol 8.27.

(MAJOR BONE *smoothing wine decanter affectionately.*)

MRS. BONE. Then go by that. They'll still be there.

BARBARA. Oh, dear ! How can I wait ? Very well, mother, I will.

MRS. BONE. Get some food and go to bed early.

BARBARA. Very well—I will—I am absolutely fagged out. (*Crosses to* BONE.) Good-night, daddy.

(*Kisses him and hands him A.B.C.*)

MAJOR BONE. Good-night, Babsy darling. (*Kisses* BARBARA.) Don't you worry, everything will be all right. Is this for me ? Oh, thanks very much. (*He keeps turning leaves over.*)

B

BARBARA. (*Crosses* L. C.) Oh, mother dear, I can't believe there is anything wrong. I do love him; we were so happy. Good-night, mother.

MRS. BONE. Good-night, dear.

(BARBARA *calls* RAWLINS *as she goes out.*)

(*After closing the door, turns at once on* BONE, *crossing* L. C.) That's it! Now we must go at once. We've just time to change and catch the night train.

MAJOR BONE. Say that again.

MRS. BONE. You'll take me down to this place to-night. (*Picking up cloak and gloves from settee* L.)

MAJOR BONE. What? I positively refuse. If you must go to-night, you go with Barbara.

(MRS. BONE *puts cloak and gloves down again.*)

MRS. BONE. And let this man wriggle out of it and get round her with lies and excuses? Not likely! By the time Barbara arrives I shall have caught him red-handed.

MAJOR BONE. What the devil do you intend doing?

MRS. BONE. I intend to go to that hotel to-night and catch him. (*Crosses* L.) I know that man, and I mean to know that woman.

MAJOR BONE. Catch them at the hotel? But they'll have gone to bed!

MRS. BONE. I know they will—that's just the point! (*Picking up cloak and gloves.*)

MAJOR BONE. Oh! So that's where you intend to walk in and catch them!

MRS. BONE. Of course it is. (*Putting on cloak.*)

MAJOR BONE. Do you mean to say you are going to burst into this woman's bedroom?

MRS. BONE. Yes!

MAJOR BONE. Oh, I see. Well, in that case, perhaps I'd better come too! (*Rising, makes a bustling movement towards the door up* C.)

(MRS. BONE *precedes him.*)

CURTAIN

SCENE 2

SCENE : *Parlour of the " Stag and Hunt " Inn, Maiden Blotton.
In the* C. *background a door giving direct access to the road
through a porch. In the back wall and* L. *of this door, windows.
The back cloth seen through these windows and also through the
door when open represents a country road. There is a door up
*R. *with glass panel, also door up* L. *with glass panel-entrances
to bar. Just below bar entrance there is a swing door, not a
complete door, leaving an aperture at the top which is the
entrance behind the counter. There is one other door down* L.
*Above front door is a window with inscription set so as to be
legible from without. It reads : " Elizabeth Spoker, Licensed
to sell by retail Beers, Wines, Spirits, Tobacco and Cigarettes,
on and off the premises." There is a window seat in alcove at
back with a green baize table in front of it. A fireplace in the*
R. *wall and a hard wooden bench running out at right angles to
it. A plain deal table is* C. *of stage, at which are placed two
stiff deal chairs with rush bottoms, one* R. *of table and the other*
L. *of table with its back to the bar door. There are one or
two similar chairs about, and a dresser with drawers standing
against the wall,* L. *The place is supposed to be illuminated by
lamplight. A lighted lamp on the wall* L. *and another larger
lamp also lighted hangs from the ceiling above the table. There
is also a light in the bar off* L. *All the blinds are down.*

(GLADYS *is discovered at the sideboard. She is preparing
a meal on a tray. She is a village girl of seventeen with
a chronic snort ; the bar door swings open rather cautiously and* ALFRED *comes into the parlour. He is an
elderly youth. He is evidently greatly attracted by
Gladys. He crosses down* L. C.)

ALFRED. Gladys !
GLADYS. Now, Alfred ! (*Turning and facing him.*) Get
back to yer bar. You know Mrs. Spoker she don't allow you
not to come into the parlour not when she's not here.
ALFRED. I reckon I'll risk she. If so be you be here.
GLADYS. (*Crosses to* C.) It's no use your coming and making

them fish-eyes at me. (*Snorts.*) They don't bear no result in my breast.

ALFRED. (*Beseechingly.*) Gladys, it ain't true that you be walking out with that ther' pig-lad o' Puddy's ?

GLADYS. (*Snort.*) Me own company's me own concern. (*Snorts—crosses* R. *with her tray.*)

ALFRED. A pig lad. Ther' be no future to he. (*Cross* C.)

GLADYS. (*At door up* R.) You get back to yer bar. I'm going up to the old lady in Number One room.

ALFRED. GLADYS !

GLADYS. (*Looking towards* C. *door.*) 'Ush ! There be someone there now. If it be Mrs. Spoker—— (*Snorts.*)

ALFRED. (*Fearfully.*) Oo ! (*Scoots back to bar door.*)

> (GLADYS *snorts scornfully and goes out* R.)
> (ALFRED *remains at bar door peering towards* C. *door.*)
> (MARGUERITE *enters* C., *carrying* PANSY, *a little dog. She is a young woman, very smart and modern, and rather authoritative. She has a slight French accent. At the moment she is very fatigued.*)

MARGUERITE. (*Seeing* ALFRED.) Oh, are you the landlord ?

ALFRED. Noo. (*At bar door.*)

MARGUERITE. Where is the landlord ?

ALFRED. At rest.

MARGUERITE. Already ?

ALFRED. Yes, 'e be the dead 'usband of the landlady !

MARGUERITE. (*Leaning on chair* R. C.) Where is the landlady ?

ALFRED. Out she be.

MARGUERITE. Well, can you attend to me ?

ALFRED. No 'm, not unless so be what you want is in the bar. I ain't allowed in 'ere.

MARGUERITE. (*Crossing* R.) Thank goodness you've got a fire, if there's nothing else. (*Warming her hands.*)

> (*Enter* PETER, *who comes down* R. C. ; *she turns to him.*)
> (PETER *is a man in the thirties, good-natured, but rather distrait and happy-go-lucky. He is carrying two bags, has a mackintosh over his shoulder and is wearing a cap.*)

PETER. (*Sees* ALFRED *in bar* L.)   What's that?
MARGUERITE.   Don't be silly—it's the barman.
PETER. (*Crossing* L.)   Barman, come out!
ALFRED.   I ain't allowed out.
PETER.   Not allowed out of the bar?
ALFRED.   No, sur.
PETER.   Oh, what a paradise! (*To* MARGUERITE.)   What have we come in here for?
MARGUERITE. (*Explanatory.*)   This is the *place.*
PETER.   The place?
MARGUERITE.   This is the place that farmer told us of.
PETER.   He said there was an hotel. (*Puts down bags* U. I.. *and closes door* U. C.)
MARGUERITE.   Well, what do you expect at a place called Maiden Blotton? A seven-course table d'hôte and a dance band? Thank goodness there's a pub at all. I'm not going to walk any further to-night. (*Sits* R. C. *at table.*)
PETER.   If you do you walk alone; on the other hand——
MARGUERITE.   What?
PETER.   Something's got to be done.
MARGUERITE.   That's very clever of you.
PETER.   Well, someone had to think of a thought. (*To* ALFRED.)   Why is this pub here?
ALFRED.   I dunno.
PETER.   Was the road built to the pub or the pub built to the road?
ALFRED.   I dunno, sur.
PETER.   He dunno. (*Moves to behind table* C.   *To* MARGUERITE.)   You ask him something. I can't cope with him, I'm too tired.
MARGUERITE.   Don't you think I'm tired? (*To* ALFRED.)   We walked three miles and met nothing. Now, what do they use this road for?
ALFRED.   I dunno.
PETER.   I think this chap's trying to be insolent. Leave this entirely in my hands. (*Authoritatively.*)   Now look here, I don't know who you think we are but we're not. We've been walking on this road for—— (*Looks at* MARGUERITE.)

MARGUERITE. Three miles.

PETER. Three miles. Look at my shoes.

(ALFRED *looks at* PETER'S *shoes*.)

Don't look at them all the time like that. Just look and carry on with the conversation, You know there's a road out there, and we know there's a road out there. What happens on this road ? Come, come, come, come, come, come !

ALFRFD. Puddy's pigs pass by 'ere.

(*Exit into bar*.)

PETER. Anyhow it's used by the best people.

MARGUERITE. Oh, I suppose we can get some food here.

PETER. I doubt it—even the pigs pass by. (*Hangs up coat* R. C.)

MARGUERITE. Anyhow, we can get some food of sorts, and then the chauffeur said he would pick us up here in the car.

PETER. But not to-night, Josephine ! (*Sitting* L. C.)

MARGUERITE. Marguerite !

PETER. I was just quoting Shakespeare.

MARGUERITE. But why can't he pick us up ?

PETER. My dear good Mrs. Hickett, did you see the radiator ?

MARGUERITE. It was only leaking, that's all.

PETER. Leaking ? It was pouring. It's dry ! You don't suppose I'd have started to walk if the car could have been repaired to-night ?

MARGUERITE. But, Peter, I thought we were just sort of walking to this place to sort of have a meal and sort of wait until the car came. (L. C.)

PETER. Then I take it you sort of gave me your luggage to sort of carry as a sort of joke.

MARGUERITE. Well, you said I'd better bring a bag in case, so I gave you two, because I thought if you carried one in each hand it would sort of balance you.

PETER. Balance me ? Look here ! (*Shows hands all stiff*.) I can't unfold my hands now.

MARGUERITE. Well, it's a good job I did bring them and Pansy too, if we're out for the night.

PETER. Out for the night ! But we can't stay here for the night. What shall we do ? (*Crosses down* L. C.)

MARGUERITE. Exactly. What shall we do ?

PETER. Ah, that's not fair. I asked you first.

MARGUERITE. (*Nodding towards bar.*) There's that man in there—call him. Be polite to him this time.

PETER. All right. Fellow creature ! (*Turns to* MARGUERITE.) That sort of brings us together.

(ALFRED *enters from bar and stands close to* PETER.)

ALFRED. Aye, sur.

(PETER *turns sharply* L. *and is startled to find himself face to face with* ALFRED.)

PETER. Have you a 'phone ?

ALFRED. What be that, sur ?

PETER. A thing you put to your ear.

ALFRED. Oh, a keyhole ?

PETER. This is a hotel all right. Have you any food or a sausage ?

ALFRED. No, sur ; not in the bar, sur.

PETER. I don't care where it is. Can we eat ?

ALFRED. I don't know, sur.

PETER. Well, damn it ! Can we try ?

(NOONY, *an old villager, very disreputable and looking like a tramp, makes a sudden dart and cautious entry from* C., *crosses* L. *to bar.*)

NOONY. Alfred !

PETER. (*Startled.*) Oh ! (*Steps back to* R. *of table* C.)

(PETER *and* MARGUERITE *look on curiously during the next few lines.*)

ALFRED. Aye, Burrt ! (*Coming out of bar.*)

NOONY. Be Mrs. Spoker in ?

ALFRED. Noo, she be gone to Downblotton.

NOONY. Then I'll go in.

ALFRED. Be careful she don't see 'ee, Burrt.

NOONY. (*Cunningly.*) Aye, just a careful 'arf tankard.

ALFRED. You best keep out of the way of she. Ye mind what she called you last time. Satan's fruit, she say.

NOONY. Aye, she be always hankering after they scriptures.
ALFRED. Well, go in, Burrt. (*Taking his arm and half pushing him in bar up* L.) Only be careful.
NOONY. Aye, a careful 'arf tankard.

(*Exit* U. L. into bar. ALFRED *dodges through swing door* L. *into bar.*)

MARGUERITE. What is all that? (L. C., *sitting.*)
PETER. (*Looking off at them.*) Some sort of secret society I think.
MARGUERITE. It's rather frightening.
PETER. I don't like that one at all. He looks like a very, very old boy scout. (*Indicates old* NOONY *in bar.*) I didn't want to come down this road at all. I suppose we'd better wait for the landlord.
MARGUERITE. Yes, but if you hadn't been quite so vague and sloppy . . . What are we going to do now?
PETER. My idea was to get to an hotel and ring up the Bunters.
MARGUERITE. And get them to send out a car.
Peter. Yes, or stay at an hotel for the night, having told the Bunters where we are.
MARGUERITE. Only you're so haphazard and piffling!
PETER. Of course I'm haphazard and piffling after what's happened, and there's poor Barbara worrying over me.
MARGUERITE. Oh, she'll be all right with the Bunters. '
PETER. Yes, but without me she won't sleep a wink. She hasn't even got my photograph.
MARGUERITE. She doesn't need your photograph, she couldn't forget a face like yours.
PETER. You needn't talk, it's a case of six of mine and half a dozen of yours.
MARGUERITE. Now we are going to be rude. It was you that got us into this mess, missing the train.
PETER. If you hadn't taken that caterpillar for a walk on the platform, I should never have seen you.
MARGUERITE. Well, you have known me long enough, you could have said " hallo " and passed on.

PETER. You're all right. Your husband thinks you are safe at the Bunters'.

MARGUERITE. My husband doesn't think—he's an M.P.

(*Sound of horse and trap off.*) Anyway, let's get some food and then find a telephone or a conveyance. (*Rises,* R. C.)

PETER. Conveyance? Where to?

MARGUERITE. The Bunters', of course. What distance is it from here to the Bunters', do you suppose? (*Cross down* R.)

(*Sound of horse and trap stops.*)

PETER. I can't go on distance-supposing, I'm fed up with it.

MARGUERITE. Well, find somebody and ask.

VOICE. (*Off.*) Goodnight to 'e, Mrs. Spoker.

MRS. SPOKER. (*Off at door* C.) Good-night, Mr. Pillbutton.

PETER. (*Looking towards door.*) Here's somebody!

(*Enter* MRS. SPOKER *from* C.)

(*Sound of horse and trap off going away.*)

(MRS. SPOKER *has an eye which gleams with sinister cal-culating suspicion. She is steeped in primitive religious principles. She has on an outdoor costume and carries an umbrella and a bag.*)

(*Pleasantly.*) Can you tell me where we can find the landlord?

MRS. SPOKER. (L. C.) Not yet, I'm his widow.

PETER. Delighted! I'm sorry. Can we stay here for a bit?

MRS. SPOKER. I am completely occupied.

PETER. I'm so sorry, of course, if you're busy. I suppose we must wait, but—er——

MRS. SPOKER. I tell you I'm completely occupied.

PETER. Oh, you mean you're full up!

MRS. SPOKER. Completely occupied.

MARGUERITE. Well—— (*She attempts to cross* L., PETER *stops her.*) Can we——

PETER. Where's the nearest hotel?

MRS. SPOKER. This is the only hotel within miles. (*Puts bag with things on dresser* L., *groceries, etc.*)

PETER. Oh, hell!

(MRS. SPOKER *starts, shocked.*)

Can we get some food ?

MRS. SPOKER. Not if you blarspheme ! (*Tin of cocoa in her hand.*)

PETER. I'm sorry, I didn't mean you to hear.

MRS. SPOKER. (*Crosses* L. C.) Whether I hear or not it all goes down in the Book.

PETER. The Book ?

PETER and MARGUERITE. (*Together.*) What book ?

MRS. SPOKER. The Book from which there is no rubbing out ! (*Crossing* L.C.)

MARGUERITE. Oh, how dreadful !

MRS. SPOKER. (*To* MARGUERITE.) I wonder you allow him to blarspheme !

MARGUERITE. Oh, I don't ; it's very disobedient of him.

MRS. SPOKER. I'm very strict here. Times may change and folks may get 'eedless in their talk and ways, but not here. This is my hotel and in it I admit only such as meets with my approval.

PETER. Then I'm surprised that you are completely occupied. (*Crosses* R., *swaggers up and down hearth with cap on.*)

MARGUERITE. That'll do, Peter. (*Crossing to* MRS. SPOKER.) Our car has broken down. We must find a night's shelter.

(PETER *takes off cap.*)

PETER. Where is the nearest town ?

MRS. SPOKER. Downblotton. Five miles on.

MARGUERITE. (*Flopping on chair* L. C.) Five miles ?

PETER. Have you a cab or a cart or an ox, or anything that is yours ?

MRS. SPOKER. No such thing.

MARGUERITE. Is there a telephone ? (*Sits* L. C.)

MRS. SPOKER. Yes, at Downblotton. (*Crosses down* L. C.)

PETER. My God !

MRS. SPOKER. Oh ! (*Drops tin of cocoa, which* MARGUERITE *picks up and hands to her.*)

PETER. My godmother lives there with some godchildren——

MARGUERITE. (*Desperately.*) Well, can we get some *food* ?

(MRS. SPOKER *gives* PETER *a freezing look.*)

MRS. SPOKER. (*Crosses down* L., *taking things from her bag and placing them on the table* D. L.) I daresay there's a drop of soup left over.

PETER. Left over from when?

MARGUERITE. Soup! All right, better than nothing. And could I have a cup of tea?

(MRS. SPOKER *taking off her gloves.*)

PETER. (*Crossing to fireplace, sits.*) And two cups of beer.

MRS. SPOKER. (*Crosses to bar and calls.*) Alfred!

ALFRED. (*Off.*) Aye, Mrs. Spoker.

MRS. SPOKER. Come you here.

(ALFRED *enters from bar* L.)

Where's Gladys?

ALFRED. Ooop. (*Indicating ceiling.*)

MRS. SPOKER. Send her to me.

ALFRED. Aye, Mrs. Spoker.

(*As* ALFRED *moves away* R., MRS. SPOKER *glances in the bar, which makes her turn quickly to* ALFRED.)

MRS. SPOKER. And, Alfred!

(*He halts.*)

MRS. SPOKER. Is that Noony I see in the bar?

ALFRED. (*Sheepishly.*) Well, you see, 'e called in, you see, for——

MRS. SPOKER. Send him to me.

ALFRED. Aye, Mrs. Spoker.

(*Exit into bar* L.)

MARGUERITE. Who is Noony? Perhaps he could help us.

MRS. SPOKER. He? He's Satan's helper.

(NOONY *with* ALFRED *enters with an air of great plausibility from the bar* U. L.)

ALFRED. (*Pushing* NOONY *out of bar.*) Go on, Burrt.

NOONY. Ah, good evening to 'ee, Mrs. Spoker.

MRS. SPOKER. (*With forefinger quivering towards* C. *exit.*) Out you go!

NOONY. But oi——

MRS. SPOKER. (*Taking him by the scruff of the neck.*) Last week you recommended this hotel to a couple living in shame. I'll teach you ! Out you go !

NOONY. Well, I thought——

MRS. SPOKER. (*Pushing* NOONY *towards exit* U. C.) You thought ! You knew ! And I know now ! Out you go !

NOONY. (*Still protesting.*) They told oi they was a-travelling together.

MRS. SPOKER. Well, if that ain't enough for you it is for me. Out you go !

NOONY. (*Going unwillingly, at the door.*) If all was like you, young folks would never get to know whether they suited !

(MARGUERITE *and* PETER *go up* C.)

MRS. SPOKER. Out you go (*pushing him*), and out you stay !

(*Exit* NOONY C., *muttering* " Bain't no harm.")
(MRS. SPOKER R. *of door.* NOONY *opens door again and calls out* " Cat ! ")

There—— (*Coming down* R. *of table* C.) You see. (*Pointedly.*) If undesirables come to my hotel, that's what they gets. (*Crosses* L. *to front of table* L. C.)

PETER. (*Crossing to* MRS. SPOKER.) What did happen on that disastrous occasion ?

MRS. SPOKER. (*Severe.*) It is not a nice subject, but a couple——

(GLADYS *appears at door* U. R., *crosses to door* D. L. *and exit.*)

comes here, just as you have come here to-night ; it was only later that I discovered that they wasn't married.

MARGUERITE. (*Crossing to* PETER.) But perhaps poor Mr. Noony thought they were only just travelling together.

MRS. SPOKER. Couples don't travel together not without shame. If I'd known it they wouldn't have stayed a moment in here. I wouldn't have risked that not in this hotel. (*Crossing* L.) I'll just see about that soup. (*Turns, pauses at door.*)

MARGUERITE. Thank you.

MRS. SPOKER. (*Crossing* R. C.) I need hardly ask whether *you* are married?

MARGUERITE. What? Of course we are married!

PETER. Yes, both of us!

MRS. SPOKER. Thank you, you'll excuse my asking, but once bit——

(*Exit* D. L.)

PETER. I wonder who bit her?

MARGUERITE. What a dreadful old thing! Anyhow, Peter, do humour her until we have had some food, if it's only soup. (*Crosses* L. C., *sits.*)

PETER. (R. C.) We wouldn't even get that if she knew we weren't husband and wife.

MARGUERITE. Just imagine if all the hotels were so particular.

PETER. Yes, Brighton beach would be one large dormitory!

MARGUERITE. I'm beginning to wonder where we shall sleep to-night.

PETER. I'll investigate. I know his name now. (*Going to bar door.*) Albert!

(ALFRED *appears at bar door.*)

ALFRED. *Alfred*, sur!

PETER. Are you sure? Oh, Alfred. (*To* MARGUERITE.) Make a note of that. (*To* ALFRED.) Tell me, is this a big village?

ALFRED. Noo, sur.

PETER. Just an ordinary village. Is there anywhere where we could put up?

ALFRED. Nowhere in the village, sur.

MARGUERITE. Not a cottage or——

ALFRED. Cottage—noo, mum. There be only fower cottages, and in them they already sleeps unhealthy in moi opinion.

MARGUERITE. Unhealthy?

ALFRED. Aye, six and seven in a bedroom mostly.

PETER. Sort of whist drive.

ALFRED. Aye, sur.

PETER. Well, get me some beer.

ALFRED. (*Turning to bar door.*) Aye, sur.

(*Exit* L.)

MARGUERITE. (*Exasperated.*) Oh, I can't walk any further to-night. (*Flopping into chair* L. *of table.*)

PETER. When I've had the beer I shall go and see if there is a light in a cottage.

> (PETER *crosses* L. *to bar.* ALFRED *hands him a tankard of beer and* PETER *goes out into bar.*)
> (MARGUERITE *at table* L. C. *nurses* PANSY.)
> (MRS. SPOKER *returns busily* D. L.)

MRS. SPOKER. Well, madam, I find much to my surprise that one of my rooms is unoccupied.

MARGUERITE. What, for the night ? (*Rises.*)

MRS. SPOKER. Yes. My maid Gladys tells me that while I was out Mr. and Mrs. Love, who were staying here, got called back home.

MARGUERITE. Oh, er—Mr. and Mrs.—Love.

MRS. SPOKER. They were staying here while their house was done up.

> (MRS. SPOKER *crosses* R. *to fireplace and puts some logs on the fire.* MARGUERITE *follows her* R.)

But Mrs. Love's mother she remained in the house, and this evening she fell over a bucket. She was walking round a ladder and failed to observe the bucket.

MARGUERITE. I see. That comes of being superstitious.

MRS. SPOKER. So Mr. and Mrs. Love were called 'ome 'urried, and my Number Two room is unoccupied.

MARGUERITE. I see—just one room ?.

MRS. SPOKER. It's a double room. So I can manage you and your husband. The maid got the room ready, thinking that I should sleep there myself.

MARGUERITE. Oh ?

MRS. SPOKER. You see, I have an old lady bedridden in Number One. And the maid thought I might wish to sleep next door.

MARGUERITE. I see. Well, I think I had really better decide to sleep here.

MRS. SPOKER. Oh, I have given orders. The maid is getting your soup and tea now. (*Crosses* L.)

MARGUERITE. Thank you *very* much. (*Sits* R. C.)

MRS. SPOKER. (*Crosses* R. C.) And as for your little dog, I'll take it to the stables.

(PETER *enters from bar.*)

MARGUERITE. Oh ! Can't she stay with me for the night ?

MRS. SPOKER. What ? Upstairs ?

MARGUERITE. Yes, of course.

MRS. SPOKER. Certainly not ! (*Crosses to table.*)

(PETER *crosses from bar carrying a pewter pot.*)

MRS. SPOKER. (*To* PETER.) That is a thing I cannot allow.

(PETER *changes beer into other hand.*)

I have no beasts in my bedroom. (*Turning to him.*)

PETER. I congratulate you ! (*Crosses up behind* MRS. SPOKER.)

MARGUERITE. Peter, madam says she's got a room for us.

PETER. What ? (*Crosses to* MARGUERITE *above table.*)

MARGUERITE. (*Grimacing at him.*) Isn't it great ?

MRS. SPOKER. Number Two room. It's a double bed !

PETER It is ? Oh, but—I——

MRS. SPOKER. Well, what now, sir ?

MARGUERITE. It's all right. Quite all right. At home we occupy separate beds, but it's quite all right.

(MARGUERITE *nudges* PETER *and he nudges* MRS. SPOKER.)

MRS. SPOKER. Ah ! Well, it is not for me to arrange people's tastes in such matters, *and* if you are in the habit of sleeping with the *dog*, madam, I don't altogether blame your husband.

(*Exit door* R.)

PETER. I say, what is all this ?

MARGUERITE. (*Rising and going up* R.) Didn't you hear her say she had a room completely unoccupied ? Do you think I was going to lose the chance ?

PETER. That's all right for you ; but what about me ?

MARGUERITE. Well, you can easily find somewhere to sleep. You can sleep in this room or in the stables with Pansy. (*Sits* R. C. *at table.*)

PETER. Why not the hen-house ?

MARGUERITE. Oh, the hen-house—don't be silly! It only means our keeping up our little deception for a night instead of a meal.

PETER. We shan't keep it up very successfully if Mrs. Spanker, or whatever her name is, finds the wife in the bedroom and the husband sharing the stables with the dog.

MARGUERITE. She won't. You can come up to my room first, and after she's gone to bed you can creep down here (*indicates* L.), and in the morning you can go out early to the car. It's very simple.

PETER. Oh, yes, without food and no bath.

MARGUERITE. Don't raise trifling difficulties. There's sure to be a pump outside.

PETER. (C.) A pump? Have you ever had a bath in a pump? (*Bus. of pretending to wash at a pump.*)

> (MARGUERITE *cuts him short.* PETER *stands by* MAR-
> GUERITE *above table as* GLADYS *enters down* L. *She
> carries a large tray on which are two plates of soup, a loaf
> of bread and knives, etc. She puts tray on dresser
> down* L.)

MARGUERITE. Are you Gladys?

GLADYS. Yes 'm. (*Snorts, crosses to table, takes cloth from drawer.*)

PETER. What's that? Oh, Gladys, how many bedrooms are there in this hotel?

GLADYS. Two, sur. Number One and Number Two. (*Laying cloth.*)

> (*Crosses to dresser* L. *for tray.*)

MARGUERITE. We're in Number Two.

PETER. (*As* MARGUERITE *sits* R. *of table* C.) What's Number One doing?

> (GLADYS *crosses to table with tray and rests it on corner*
> D. L.)

MARGUERITE. There's an old lady in there bedridden, isn't there?

GLADYS. Yes 'm, she's got—— (*Snorts, putting soup on table.*)

PETER. That must be very painful.

MARGUERITE. You're bringing me some tea, aren't you?
GLADYS. Yes 'm, it's ready. (*Snorts.*)
PETER. (*Looking after* GLADYS.) Sounds like her bed-time.

(*Exit* GLADYS *down* L., *leaving door open.*)

MARGUERITE. Peter, don't ask questions that rouse suspicion. (*Takes mouthful of soup.*) Oh, that's good!
PETER. (*Taking mouthful of soup.*) Yes, mox-tail.
MARGUERITE. Cut the bread and pass the salt.

(PETER *cuts the bread and hands a piece to her.*)

I don't mind about deceiving this landlady. If people are so narrow-minded—— (*Taking bread.*) Thanks.
PETER. No, but I wonder what poor Barbara will think.
MARGUERITE. You must explain, that's all. She'll understand. Salt, please.
PETER. Got all you want?
MARGUERITE. For the moment.
PETER. See you later. (*Eats soup busily.*)
MARGUERITE. It does sound silly, I know, but with this completely occupied landlady——
PETER. We daren't tell her anything. She'd turn us out like a shot. (*He puts a small piece of bread underneath his plate which tilts the soup to one side.*)
MARGUERITE. I hope your wife will be quite reasonable.
PETER. My wife's a darling.
MARGUERITE. I'm so looking forward to meeting her.
PETER. But she has a mother.
MARGUERITE. Oh! (*Laughing.*)
PETER. Oh, a beauty. She's the head of the Cross Word Mother-in-Law Society. Her father's all right. He's a great sport—a sort of wet accumulator.
MARGUERITE. Well, your mother-in-law mustn't know, that's all.

(*Enter* GLADYS *down* L. *She snorts as she carries a cup of tea and places it down on table* R. ALFRED *appears at swing door, watching* GLADYS.)

PETER. I never let her know a thing. What's that?

C

GLADYS. (*Above table to* PETER.) Will there be anything more, sur ?

PETER. (*Thoughtfully.*) Anything more. What is there ?

GLADYS. Nothing !

PETER. Oh, then there will be nothing more.

GLADYS. Oh, I believe there be some chaise.

PETER. What kind of chaise ?

(GLADYS *snorts.*)

Well, bring me some more beer.

(*Exit* GLADYS *to bar with tankard.*)

MARGUERITE. I didn't know what chaise meant at first.

PETER. She means cheese ; it's a very old Cheshire word.

MARGUERITE. (*Annoyed.*) Peter, do you want *all* your soup ?

PETER. I think so. Why ?

MARGUERITE. (*Still drinking soup.*) I wanted some for Pansy.

PETER. What about yours ?

MARGUERITE. I need that. I walked three miles.

PETER. I walked three miles and two bags.

MARGUERITE (*to* PANSY.) Never mind, darling, you shall have some milk.

PETER. What worries me about Barbara is——

(MRS. SPOKER *enters from down* L.)

MARGUERITE. (*Hoarsely.*) She'll be all right——

MRS. SPOKER. (*Crossing to* L. C.) I think I'll take the dog now, madam.

MARGUERITE. Oh, can't she stay with me until I go to bed ?

MRS. SPOKER. Well, I take it you won't be long now. We keep early hours here.

PETER. (*Turning to* MRS. SPOKER.) Give us a chance, I've ordered some more beer.

MRS. SPOKER. You can't sit up all night drinking beer, sir !

PETER. Can't I !

MARGUERITE. I shall turn in quite soon. (*Looks at* PETER *meaningly and tries to conciliate* MRS. SPOKER.)

MRS. SPOKER. Very well. (*To* PETER.) And there will be the register to sign.

PETER. The what? (*Startled.*)
MARGUERITE. (*Drinking tea, calmly.*) Yes, of course.
MRS. SPOKER. I'll get the book. (*Crosses* L. *to table.*) What name, please?
MARGUERITE. Name?
PETER. Oh, the name—you've got it! (*To* MARGUERITE.)
MARGUERITE. Hickett.
PETER. Hickett, Hickett.
MRS. SPOKER. Rikki-Tikki?
PETER. I've got hiccoughs. Hickett. I said so twice. (*Sits* `L. *of table* C.)
MRS. SPOKER. But why say so twice? That's what I didn't understand.

(*Voice heard off.*)

SLOLEY-JONES. (*Off.*) Oh dear! Oh dear, dear!
MRS. SPOKER. (*Turning sharply.*) See who that is, Gladys!

(GLADYS *goes up and investigates.*)

MARGUERITE. Very good soup, Mrs. Spoker.
MRS. SPOKER. Thank you, madam.
GLADYS. (*From up stage* C.) The Rev. Sloley-Jones.
MRS. SPOKER. Oh, what a nuisance that man is!

(MARGUERITE'S *face suddenly becomes animated, but not with pleasure. She glances at* PETER *and crosses* R. *as* SLOLEY-JONES *enters. He is in cycling overalls, with waterproof cape, motor gloves, and cap, and wears a clerical collar.*)

SLOLEY-J. (*In a hearty voice.*) By Jove! I've had a terrible time to-night. Good evening, Mrs. Spoker.
MRS. SPOKER. And what do you want, sir? I'm completely occupied.
SLOLEY-J. Well (*coming down* L.), as a matter of absolute fact, I looked in to see whether I could get you to give me a little oil. I want oiling.
MRS. SPOKER. Well, you can't come 'ere this time of night and get oiled.

SLOLEY-J. (*Suddenly seeing* MARGUERITE.) Why, good gracious alive ! How do you do ?

(SLOLEY-J. *puts his hand out, and* PETER, *rising, attempts to shake it, but* SLOLEY-J. *crosses over to* MARGUERITE. PETER *goes up to bar and shakes hands with* ALFRED.)

Surely it is Mrs. Hickett ?

MARGUERITE. (*Cordially.*) Why, Mr. Sloley-Jones !

SLOLEY-J. It is Hickett, the name, isn't it ? First time we've met, you know, since you got married. (*Shaking hands with* MARGUERITE.) Awfully sorry I couldn't be at your wedding. But fancy meeting you here, though !

MARGUERITE. Yes, we're on our way to the Bunters'. Are you staying at the Bunters' ?

SLOLEY-J. No—oh, no ! But I always spend my leave in these parts, you know. I'm just on a holiday.

MARGUERITE. Our car broke down and we came here.

SLOLEY-J. Oh, bad luck ! (*Turning to* PETER.) And this, of course, is your husband !

(PETER *turns his back on* SLOLEY-J. *and crouches up* L. *to bar and comes down again* L.)

(*Wringing* PETER'S *hand.*) First time we've met, isn't it ?

PETER. I hope so !

MARGUERITE. (*To* PETER.) Peter, this is Mr. Jones, you know.

PETER. Oh, Jones, of course, I've heard the name.

SLOLEY-J. I'm so delighted to meet you. How do you do ? Splendid ! How are you ? (*Shakes hands again.*)

PETER. Not at all, are you ?

SLOLEY-J. Oh, I'm very well, thanks, except that I'm having a good deal of trouble with my motor-bike. That's why I stopped here. I'm very overheated. However, an ill wind, you know. I'm awfully bucked to come across you like this. Of course, I've heard a great deal about you.

PETER. About me ? Oh, surely not !

SLOLEY-J. Oh, yes ; come now ! (*Laughing.*) A man like you can't hope to remain in obscurity.

PETER. I never remain there long. I'm gone like a shot.

(PETER *and* MRS. SPOKER *exchange looks.*)

SLOLEY-J. I've followed your career in the House.

PETER. Oh, you mustn't follow me about like that.

MARGUERITE. But my husband's got a holiday from his politics just now.

SLOLEY-J. Mind you, I don't see eye to eye with all you preach. Over this question of housing, now, I can't say that I altogether agree with your attitude.

PETER. No—er—I don't feel very happy about it myself. (*Looks at* MRS. SPOKER.)

SLOLEY-J. Aha! I don't suppose you'd admit that in the House.

(MRS. SPOKER *closes up towards Peter.*)

PETER. No, not in the house. I just do it outside and come back again.

SLOLEY-J. (*Gushingly.*) Well, I suppose with all said and done there is an awful lot of deception goes on ?

PETER. Oh, rather ! Yes, we have a lot of fun !

(*Bus.:* PETER *puts his hand round* MRS. SPOKER'S L. *shoulder, and before she has time to look round he has exchanged places with* SLOLEY-JONES. MRS. SPOKER *looks very indignantly at* SLOLEY-JONES, *who cannot understand her attitude.*)

SLOLEY-J. (*Turning to* MARGUERITE.) I'm delighted to meet your husband in such candid mood, Mrs. Hickett. Well, I suppose I'd better be pushing off. (*Crossing* L.) That is, if you're sure I can't get what I want here.

(PETER *crosses* R., MARGUERITE C.)

MRS. SPOKER. Quite sure. It's after hours in any case. And you can't stay here. I have just let my last room to Mr. and Mrs. Hickett.

MARGUERITE. (*Crosses* L. C., *to* JONES.) Where are you staying, Mr. Jones ?

SLOLEY-J. Downblotton's my headquarters. Of course I'd go on to the Bunters' at Rushcombe, and let Lady Bunter know about you——

Marguerite and Peter. Oh, no, no, thank you! That is very kind of you!

Sloley-J. No? Well, perhaps it's just as well, because I don't suppose I shall get even as far as Downblotton, let alone Rushcombe. I do wish I'd got thoroughly oiled before I started.

Mrs. Spoker. Well, you can't come back here, whatever happens.

Sloley-J. Dear, dear me, then we must hope for the best. Good-night, Mrs. Hickett—good—— (*Breaking off.*) Oh, I say, hallo, by Christopher! what a nice little dog. Your little dog, Mrs. Hickett?

(Mrs. Spoker *crosses up* c. *to door.*)

Marguerite. (*With forced politeness.*) Yes.

Sloley-J. (*Patting* Pansy.) Dear little dog, nice little dog! (*Holding his right hand out in front of him.*) Pretty little dog. Good-night, little dog!

Peter. Good-night, little man! (*Taking his hand and crossing* l.)

(Mrs. Spoker *has gone up to door, which she holds open, clearing her throat. It is obvious that everyone wants* Sloley-J. *to go.*)

Sloley-J. (*Turning to door.*) Well, well, I suppose I shan't be quite so hot by this time. Good-night—er—all!

(Peter *crosses* c. *in front of table.*)

(*With a final chuckle of sociability* Sloley-Jones *goes.*)

(Mrs. Spoker *closes the door and comes down* r.)

Mrs. Spoker. (*To* Peter.) And so you are a member of the House of Parliament?

Marguerite. (*Readily.*) Yes, my husband is in the House.

Mrs. Spoker. And which side may you be on?

Peter. Well, you know, as you come in, I'm just on the right.

Mrs. Spoker. Yes, but are you for or against the brewers?

Peter. I'm for the brewers!

Mrs. Spoker. Hum, well, I'll get the register. (*Crosses* l.) Perhaps when you sign your name you'll kindly put M.P. after it, it may be an object of interest in these parts.

(*Exit down* l.)

PETER. This is terrible! Who is the person? He knows you!

MARGUERITE. Oh, his name is Sloley-Jones.

PETER. I don't care whether it's Quickly-Smith.

MARGUERITE. He is harmless. I'll make it all right with him when I see him again. He won't remember you.

PETER. Won't he? I know those little fussy men. (*Pacing stage* L.) They never forget things they should forget. And what about this register? I can't sign your husband's name!

MARGUERITE. Of course you can!

PETER. But it's forgery, and that's a thing I very seldom do.

(MRS. SPOKER *returns with register, also pen and ink-bottle, which she puts on the table* L. C.)

MRS. SPOKER. If you'll kindly make the entry now, sir?

MARGUERITE. And are you going to take the dog? (*Rising.*)

MRS. SPOKER. Certainly.

MARGUERITE. I'm going up to my room now if you'll please take her at once.

MRS. SPOKER. Yes, give her to me.

MARGUERITE. (*Surrendering* PANSY.) I hope she won't howl.

MRS. SPOKER. (*Crossing in front of table* C.) It won't make any difference if she do howl. She won't be heard from the stables.

(PETER *crosses up* R. C. *and opens door for* MRS. SPOKER.)
(*She goes out up* R. *with dog.*)

MARGUERITE. What a sweet face!

PETER. Whose?

MARGUERITE. Pansy's.

PETER. (*Who has taken pen and is regarding register dismally.*) Look here, Marguerite, this won't do—I mean about this book.

MARGUERITE. That's exactly why I got rid of Mrs. Spoker. I'll sign it.

PETER. (*Passing book, giving her pen.*) I think you'd better.

MARGUERITE. (*Preparing to inscribe.*) Mr. and Mrs. Hickett, you see. I'm Mrs. Hickett, aren't I? You can't be run in for half a forgery, can you?

PETER. Go on, then. Mr. Hickett, M.P., remember. (*Enter* GLADYS D. L.)

MARGUERITE. And Mrs. Hickett.

(*While* MARGUERITE *is writing and he is looking over her shoulder at the book,* GLADYS *comes in down* L., *quietly, and crosses to sideboard, collects groceries and puts them inside bag.*)

Room number?

(GLADYS *snorts.*)

(*Glancing up at* GLADYS.) Number Two, isn't it?

GLADYS. 'Sright. (*Takes bag of groceries from sideboard* L. *and exit* D. L.)

PETER. What's that?

MARGUERITE. That is right.

PETER. Oh, short cut.

MARGUERITE. (*To him.*) I'd better put my address.

PETER. Put any address you like, only don't put mine.

MARGUERITE. I shall put " London."

(*Door bangs off* R. MARGUERITE *quickly passes book over to* PETER, *who starts to write.* MARGUERITE *spells* " London " *for him.*)

(MRS. SPOKER *re-enters* R. *and comes straight over and examines his handiwork.*)

MRS. SPOKER. H'm, you don't write very clear.

PETER. I've just had some very thick soup.

(MRS. SPOKER *tries to see what is written.*)

MRS. SPOKER. (*Closing book and taking it with ink-pot, etc., and turning to* MARGUERITE.) Would you care for a fire in your room? Mrs. Love used to have one and it is laid.

MARGUERITE. Yes, I think it would be very welcome.

MRS. SPOKER. Very well, then. (*At bar door, calling.*) Alfred!

ALFRED. (*In bar off.*) Aye, Mrs. Spoker!

MRS. SPOKER. Come you here. (*Crosses* L. *of table* C.)

(*Enter* ALFRED L.)

Take you those two bags up to Number Two and show Mr. and Mrs. Hickett the way. And put a light to the fire.

MARGUERITE. (*Taking her coat from bench.*)   I think I'll go up to my room now.   Good-night, Mrs. Spoker.

MRS. SPOKER.   Good-night to you, madam.

PETER. (*Fatuously.*)   Shall I come up too, dear ?

MRS. SPOKER.   Yes, please.

PETER.   Er—I was talking to my wife.

MRS. SPOKER.   And the sooner the house is quiet the better.

MARGUERITE.   Come along then, Peter.

(*Exit door* U. R.)

PETER.   All right.

(PETER *pretends to be in a great hurry.   Feels seat of bench* U. L., *then goes to fireplace and warms his* R. *hand, which he holds up as he goes towards door* U. R., *goes back to fireplace and warms his left hand which he also holds up, then attempts to go, but finds himself on the wrong side of the door.   MRS. SPOKER'S attention is drawn to his foolishness.*)

MRS. SPOKER. (*Cross to table* L.)   You'll be wanting a candle.

PETER.   Yes, I expect I shall.

(MRS. SPOKER *goes to sideboard and gets candle in a stick, which she hands to* PETER.)

I shall take great care of it !   (*Hugs candle.*)   The bedroom is on the next floor, isn't it ?   (R. C.)   The one above this.

MRS. SPOKER.   It is.

PETER.   And the bedridden old lady, is she also on the same floor ?   (*Closing register on table* C.)

MRS. SPOKER.   Next door to you, so please observe as much quiet as possible.

PETER.   Oh, I shan't take any notice of her at all.   Where do you sleep, Mrs. Spicer ?

MRS. SPOKER.   And *why* do you want to know ?

PETER.   Ah, did I say that ?   I don't want to know.   I thought that the old lady next door might——

MRS. SPOKER.   On the same floor, but up a different flight of stairs.   Don't you try and find your way about because it is not easy.   I shall hear you if you call.

PETER.   Yes, I'm not likely to call you, to—er—call on you, to—er—yes, all right.

(ALFRED *returns* R.)

ALFRED.   (*As* PETER *crosses.*)   Can you find your way, sur ?
PETER.   I think so, Albert.   Your mother has just told me.

(*During dialogue between* PETER *and* ALFRED, MRS. SPOKER *clears table of register, pen and ink and puts them on dresser, then*—
Exit into bar with tankard.)

ALFRED.   The door facing 'ee, sur, on the first landing.
PETER.   Ah, yes.
ALFRED.   Good-night to 'ee, sur.
PETER.   What's that ?
ALFRED.   Good-night to 'ee.
PETER.   Oh, do that, will you ?

(*Exit up* R.)
(MRS. SPOKER *re-enters from bar to table* C.)

MRS. SPOKER.   Well, Alfred, did you light the fire in Number Two ?
ALFRED.   Aye, Mrs. Spoker.
MRS. SPOKER.   And have you locked the bar door ?
ALFRED.   Aye, Mrs. Spoker.
MRS. SPOKER.   And seen to the bar windows ?   (*Getting on chair* L. *of table.*)
ALFRED.   Aye, Mrs. Spoker.
MRS. SPOKER.   And locked the cash drawer in the bar ?
ALFRED.   Aye.
MRS. SPOKER.   Where is the key ?   (*Gets on top of table.*)
ALFRED.   (*Producing key from pocket.*)   'Ere she be.
MRS. SPOKER.   Have you done all those things that you ought to have done ?
ALFRED.   Aye, Mrs. Spoker.
MRS. SPOKER.   (*Severely.*)   And have you left undone those things that you ought *not* to have done ?
ALFRED.   Aye, Mrs. Spoker.

MRS. SPOKER. Then you can go to bed. (*Puts out hanging lamp.*)

(MRS. SPOKER *gets down from table.*)

ALFRED. Aye, Mrs. Spoker.

(*Exit door* L.)

(MRS. SPOKER *takes key and locks door* U. C., *turns out lamp outside bar, exit to bar and puts out small lamp inside bar.*)

(*The stage is now in darkness excepting for the glow from the fire.*)

(PETER *is seen on landing through glass door up* R., *stealing quietly down the stairs carrying a lighted candle and a blanket over his arm. He opens the door cautiously and makes his way* D. R. *towards* C. MRS. SPOKER *re-enters from bar carrying a small lamp. She sees* PETER *and at once shades the light from her lamp by putting her hand in front of it. She comes down* L. *in front of table, and taking her hand away from lamp confronts* PETER. PETER, *obviously surprised, exclaims.*)

PETER. Hallo!

MRS. SPOKER. What are you doing here, sir?

PETER. (*At a loss for what to say.*) I'm looking for a melon.

MRS. SPOKER. (*Incredulously.*) A melon! (*Then, seeing blanket.*) What may you be doing with that blanket? (*Down* L. C.)

PETER. Oh, the blanket! Oh, yes, it was *you* I wanted to see. I was going to ask you if you would slip out to the stables and wrap the little dog in the little blanket.

MRS. SPOKER, What? In my best blanket!

PETER. Is this your best blanket? I thought it was the other one. Never mind. Good-night. (*Blows candle out.*) Oh! (*Lights candle again.*) Sorry, I thought I'd gone; it doesn't matter.

MRS. SPOKER. Doesn't matter?

PETER. I mean about the little dog. (*Moving slightly towards door* R.) He'll be all right.

MRS. SPOKER. He'll have to be.

PETER. Yes, that's what I said to him the day before yesterday.
I said you'll have to be all right. He only just barked, and I
wagged my tail, and then we were both happy. Now you go
straight to bed like a good little girl. We know what dogs are, so
she'll be all right.

MRS. SPOKER. I thought you said it was a he.

PETER. It was, but not now.

(*He goes out and closes door* R. *He is seen disappearing
up the stairs.*)

(MRS. SPOKER *stands for a moment staring after him.*)

MRS. SPOKER. Well !

(*She makes a movement towards door* D. L. *She can be
seen to have an inspiration. She goes to the door* R.,
*locks it on the inside, and takes the key. This with the
key that* ALFRED *has given her and the door key of the
inn, she takes with her, crosses* D. L. *Pause, looks across
to door* R. *and with a satisfied look exit* D. L.)

PETER'S *shadow is again seen through the glass door, making
his way down the stairs. He reaches the door, tries the
handle gently, but of course the door will not open. He
looks close into the lock, and realises the situation.
Rattling the handle furiously the silhouette of his head
is clearly seen as he says "* Damn ! "

CURTAIN

ACT II

SCENE : *Number Two room of the " Stag and Hunt." The room is small. A large proportion of it is occupied by a big double bed. This has its head up the R. wall and with a small table up stage occupies the whole of this side of the stage. The one door to the room is in the centre background. L. of the door a towel rail, U. L. of the door the fireplace. A window up stage in the L. wall. A washing-stand down stage against the L. wall. A roller-blind hangs over the window. A lamp on a chair by the bed R. The jug is out of the basin on the washing-stand, but has not been placed on the floor. A toothbrush in the customary receptacle like a vase, on the washing-stand. A pair of bedroom slippers is beneath the bed. On the wall above the bed a picture of lovers. On the wall above small table a picture of a soul being escorted by angels. Above the fireplace another picture of a sailor and little girl. A trunk at the foot of the bed, suitcase alongside. A chair by the window. A suitcase on chair L. of bed.*

(MARGUERITE *is sitting up in bed reading a novel. She is in a very pretty and becoming negligée. There is a faint and nervous tapping at the door.* MARGUERITE *lowers her novel and looks in that direction.*)

MARGUERITE. (*Sits up.*) Come in.

(*Knocking is repeated.* PETER *pushes his head through door* C. *He still carries a lighted candle and a blanket. He closes the door.*)

Oh, it's you. What's the matter with *you* ?

PETER. (*Softly, in a voice of one keeping a firm control over his feelings.*) I cannot sleep in the parlour. (*At door.*)

MARGUERITE. Oh, nonsense, Peter ; you can't have tried. You've only *been* there ten minutes.

PETER. I tell you I can't sleep in the parlour.

MARGUERITE. Why not ?

PETER. Because I can't get in—it's locked.

MARGUERITE. Well, come in. Where have you been all the time then?

(PETER *comes down to foot of bed.*)

PETER. I haven't been anywhere all the time. But I've been everywhere one can, and where one can one can't sleep.

MARGUERITE. What about the back door downstairs?

PETER. (*Heartily.*) I've been through there.

· MARGUERITE. Where does that lead to?

PETER. To the back. Hence the expression—back door. (*Crosses down* L.)

MARGUERITE. Can't you sleep there?

PETER. How do you mean, sleep *there*? In the aperture of the back door? *Behind* the back door. Swinging on the back door to rock myself to sleep?

MARGUERITE. Isn't there anything through the back door?

PETER. A sink. Oh, and a pump. You were quite right about the pump. (*Crosses to foot of bed.*) But if I remember rightly, that was for the morning.

MARGUERITE. What about the stables?

PETER. I tested the stables.

MARGUERITE. Did you go into the stables?

PETER. (*Crosses* D. R., *puts candle on the mantelpiece.*) One doesn't have to. I tested them from the back door. (*Warms hands by fire. Has blanket over his arm.*)

MARGUERITE. I hope Pansy is all right.

PETER. (*Looking over shoulder.*) Oh, she's all right. I think she's getting some ratting.

MARGUERITE. Oh, Peter, was she howling?

PETER. She's perfectly all right. We are not discussing Pansy. We are discussing me. And I am anything but perfectly all right.

MARGUERITE. I suppose you can't sleep on the stairs?

PETER. You're right. I've tried the stairs, and I cannot sleep thereon.

MARGUERITE. Well, there must be somewhere.

PETER. I've been through every door there is that isn't locked, even the bedridden old lady's.

MARGUERITE.   Good heavens !   What happened ?

PETER.   Nothing.   She just cocked an eye at me and murmured " Eno's."

MARGUERITE.   My dear Peter, I'm frightfully sorry, but I really don't see what can be done.

PETER.   (*Crosses* U. C., D. L., U. L., and D. C.)   The architecture of this place is all wrong.   The parlour's locked, the kitchen's locked ; there's no way to the bar, otherwise I'd go and do a bit of moaning at the bar.   I appear to be condemned to wander about the house all night, like a lost soul with a candle and a blanket.   (*Pause, looks at* MARGUERITE.)   I'd give anything for a bed like yours.

MARGUERITE.   Then you can't be hard to please.   It goes up and down in the middle like the hump of a camel.   Only it does it twice.   That's a dromedary, isn't it ?

PETER.   I should think that must be rather restful, if you work yourself into the right position.

MARGUERITE.   I can tell you if you're keen on a bed like this you'd take to the stables like a duck to water.

(PETER *crosses* L. *to window and looks out.*)

PETER.   It is raining, by the way.

MARGUERITE.   Is it ?

PETER.   Oh, terrible night.   It's pouring all over the place.

MARGUERITE.   Oh, I hope the stables are watertight.

PETER.   Look here.   (*Crosses to foot of bed.*)   I am not going to the stables.   That's definite.

MARGUERITE.   No, I was thinking of Pansy.

(*A sharp rapping on the door outside and* MRS. SPOKER'S *voice is heard.*)

MRS. SPOKER.   (*Off.*)   Silence in there, please !

(PETER *crosses right to fireplace.*)
It is high time everyone was in bed and asleep.

PETER.   All right.   I know that.

MRS. SPOKER.   (*Off.*)   Then let me have no more of it.   The old lady is not well.   And in any case I cannot have a disturbance in my hotel.   So kindly get into bed, without further noise.

PETER.   All right, all right.

MARGUERITE. He'll be in bed in a minute.
MRS. SPOKER. (*Off.*) So I should hope.

(*A pause.* PETER *goes up to the door and listens, then returns to above bed.*)

PETER. Well, keep on hoping. That settles it. It was bad enough before. . . . Upstairs and downstairs in my old lady's bedridden chamber. And now every landing I go on to, I shall meet this horrible old thing in night attire—awful.
MARGUERITE. Look here, Peter. (*She sits up a little higher in bed and speaks in a most practical voice.*) There is only one thing to be done.
PETER. What's that? (*At foot of bed.*)
MARGUERITE. You can take this pillow and get down on the floor with your blanket and go to sleep.
PETER. (*Hesitating.*) What?
MARGUERITE. (*Taking second pillow and throwing it at foot of bed.*) Go on—that'll settle it.
PETER. Yes. It very likely will.
MARGUERITE. What d'you mean?
PETER. Well, do you think it's wise?
MARGUERITE. You keep grousing because you've got nowhere to sleep. Go on. Sleep on the floor.
PETER. Suppose anyone found out.
MARGUERITE. The only people who will find out will find out because we shall tell them. To any decent-minded person there's nothing wrong in your sleeping on the floor of my room, is there?
PETER. Yes, but where's the decent-minded person?
MARGUERITE. My husband hasn't got a nasty mind. Has your wife got a nasty mind?
PETER. No, but she's got a nasty mother.
MARGUERITE. Oh, all right. I was only trying to help. Go to the stables if you like.

(*Both grab at pillow at foot of bed.* PETER *gets pillow and walks away* L.)

PETER. No, I daresay it's all right. Only you know what some people are. If they heard I'd stayed in your room all night, they'd be on us like bees on a queen or a drone or whatever it is bees get on to.

MARGUERITE.   Look here, Peter, *I* don't want you in my room in the least bit, I'm only thinking of you.   And if you stand there arguing that old woman is sure to come back.

PETER.   You're right.

MARGUERITE.   Well, of course I'm right.

PETER.   All right, then—I said all right, then.

MARGUERITE.   All right—All right.

PETER.   I'll risk it.

MARGUERITE.   Risk what ?

PETER.   (*Mumbling.*)   Sleeping on the floor of your room.

MARGUERITE.   Oh !

PETER.   (*With a survey of the floor.*)   After all, the floor is no bed of roses.   (*Drops pillow and blanket on floor and loosens collar and tie.*)   Up C. *to door, stoops with his handkerchief at bottom of door* C., *draught blows it out.   Picks pillow and blanket up after handkerchief business.*)   There is an absolute Arctic blast blowing in under this door !

MARGUERITE.   You can get well in the corner under the washing-stand.   You'll be all right there.

PETER.   (*Crossing* L.—*testing with his hand for draught at washstand.*)   On the contrary the wind is blowing straight into the washing-stand.

MARGUERITE.   Hurry up and don't footle about.

PETER (*Throws blanket and pillow on floor* C., *takes coat off and carries it on arm.   Annoyed.*)   Well, dash it all, if I've got to sleep on the floor, you might let me pick my own pitch.   I can't lie on a floor all night in the teeth of a gale.   I shall die. (*Throws his collar into the wash-stand basin, snatches it up quickly and shakes imaginary water off it.   He then puts collar on washing-stand, crosses to foot of bed.*)

MARGUERITE.   You can lie with your feet under the bed, if you like.

PETER.   (*He continues to investigate for draughts.*)   That's very extraordinary.

MARGUERITE.   What is ?

PETER.   There's a three-cornered blast.

D

MARGUERITE. Go on, hurry up and get settled.

PETER. It doesn't matter much where I go. I shall die. (C., *puts coat on.*)

MARGUERITE. Well, if you've never had anything worse happen to you than have to spend a night on the floor of an inn——

PETER. Yes, but what an inn ! (*Tapping floor with knuckles.*) And what a floor ! You're all right—here, above the draughts. (*Crosses up* C., *gazing at picture of the soul on wall.*) That'd be me. (*Pointing to picture.*)

> (MARGUERITE *looks at picture and smiles.*)
> (*Bus. of wing flapping with elbows.*)
> (PETER *picks blanket, etc., from* C., *crosses to washstand, puts them down, takes coat off and puts it over chair.*)

You will find my body 'neath the shade of the old washing-stand.

> (*Wrapping himself round in the blanket, he gets down very awkwardly on the floor, near leg of washing-stand, which he bumps with his head down stage.* PETER *props pillow against leg of washing-stand down stage, and keeps pressing both sides of pillow, which makes it bulge at top corner, which he knocks down. Repeat pillow bus.* PETER *kneels down and rests his head on the pillow but his arms are in the way. He puts his right arm behind him, then left arm, then both, but is unable to get comfortably settled.* PETER *has great difficulty in getting under washing-stand.*
> MARGUERITE *has resumed her book.* PETER *wriggles a good deal. After a few moments he exclaims in an altered tone of genuine misery.*)

Oh, how uncomfortable this is !

MARGUERITE. Why don't you try lying the other way round ?

PETER. That's not a bad idea.

> (PETER *does so, putting pillow up stage, lies underneath washing-stand and gets feet entangled with chair. His head is up stage.*)

I'm round.

MARGUERITE.   Is that better?

PETER.   Better than what?

MARGUERITE.   Oh, Peter, would you mind blowing out this candle?

(*Rain starts.*)

(PETER *tries to blow out candle from under washstand twice.*)

PETER.   I can't reach it.

MARGUERITE.   Well, just jump up and do it.

PETER.   (*Struggling to his feet, bumps head, and catches his foot in chair. Crosses* R., *blanket on head.*)   I wish you'd think of things in their proper order.

(*He blows out the candle on mantelpiece, which he snuffs and burns his fingers, and attempts to put the lamp out, but* MARGUERITE *stops him.*)

MARGUERITE.   No, I'll keep this one until I've finished reading.

PETER.   (*Crossing.*)   Back to the old four-poster.   Now remember, no more of this just jumping up business.

(PETER *kneels on the mat, slips and bumps his chin on floor.*)

MARGUERITE.   Peter, do you mean to say your wife never thinks of things at night and sends you out of bed?

PETER.   Certainly not.   And don't remind me of my wife. (*Lying down. He is on the floor again and settles himself.*)   Oh, how I love my wife!   (*Brief pause.*)   Oh, I do love her, little darling.   (*Loudly.*)   Blast this blanket.   If I pull it down I get a draught, and if I pull it up it tickles my neck ; oh, utterly blast and curse this night!

(PETER *groans twice. He holds on to top of washstand, but his hand drops and his elbow knocks the floor.*)

Oh, how I hate washing-stands!

MARGUERITE.   Oh, Peter, do keep quiet.   I'm going to try and get some sleep now.   Oh, Peter, I'm sorry I forgot.   Would you mind opening the window?

PETER.   Open the window!   Do you *want* me to die?

MARGUERITE.   We must have air.

PETER. I've got some, thanks.

MARGUERITE. If we don't have it open I shall have such a headache in the morning.

PETER. I've got one now. (*Puts blanket over his head.*)

MARGUERITE. If you won't do it, I must try again myself.

PETER. No, no, Marguerite, you mustn't get out of bed. Where are you? (*Struggles to get out.*) I'll do it. (*Puts coat on. He gets up again and goes to window.*) A little walk will bring the blood back to my feet.

> (PETER *releases blind, which flies up. He pulls it down again and releases it two or three times—enjoying it, looks round at* MARGUERITE, *smiling.*)

MARGUERITE. (*Severely.*) Open the window, can't you?

PETER. (*Trying.*) No.

MARGUERITE. There's a catch somewhere.

PETER. Yes, I think there is.

MARGUERITE. (*Sitting up in bed.*) That's right—that's right. Pull it down from the top.

PETER. I can't pull down from the top.

MARGUERITE. Then push it up from the bottom.

> (*He pushes up window, which opens suddenly and almost falls out. Moves down* L.)

That's too wide, now. Won't it stay half-way open?

PETER. (*Tries to move window.*) I can't move it at all now.

MARGUERITE. Well, never mind, leave it—leave it.

> (PETER *sits on chair to operate blind again; it flies up. He does blind bus. two or three times, then turns round and smiles at* MARGUERITE.)

Leave that blind alone and get back to bed.

PETER. Isn't it time to get up yet? (*Takes off coat and hangs it on chair* L.) Bed! I'm sick of that spot. (*Looking round room.*) I'm going to find a fresh position.

> (PETER *crosses to fireplace* L.)

MARGUERITE. Why didn't you think of that place before? It's much warmer there.

PETER. I can't argue at this time of night.

(PETER *crosses over to fireplace—throws down blanket and
pillow and lies down, head near fireplace—feet up stage.
Chimney smokes—he puts his head in coal scuttle—after
the second draught he crawls towards trunk* C.)

MARGUERITE. Peter, I believe the chimney is going to smoke.

PETER. Watson, you surpass yourself.

MARGUERITE. It's caused by that window. You'll have to
lie somewhere else.

PETER. I'm not going to lie under the window, I can tell you
that.

(MARGUERITE *makes herself comfortable. She takes up
her book again and starts to read.* PETER *settles himself
against trunk, blanket over his head. Suddenly there
comes the sound of* PANSY *howling outside. At first it
passes unnoticed.*)

(MARGUERITE *lowers her book and raises her head, listens.
She starts to read again. Two dog howls.*)

MARGUERITE. Peter, it's Pansy. Can't you hear her?

PETER. (*Emphatically.*) No!

(*Dog howl.*)

MARGUERITE. Peter, you know it's Pansy. Oh, please go
down and fetch her, will you?

PETER. No, thank you.

MARGUERITE. I know if you were Claude you'd go down and
get her in.

PETER. If I were Claude I shouldn't have cramp in my spine.

(*Dog howl.*)

MARGUERITE. Oh, Peter, please!

PETER. I can't move my right leg. It is numb-a. All my
right side is more or less numb-a. I can't do that. (*Opens and
shuts right hand.*)

(*Dog howl.*)

MARGUERITE. Poor little girl!

PETER. She can't be worse off than I am.

MARGUERITE. Yes, but somehow it's much more pathetic in
a dog.

PETER. And here am I, a human being—— (*Desperately, getting up.*)

MARGUERITE. Peter, have you no regard for dumb animals ? (*Dog howls loudly.*)

PETER. (*Indicating dog—throws clothing* D. C.) Yes, when they *are* dumb-a.

MARGUERITE. Well, you can easily get to the stables. You said so yourself. (*Dog howl.*)

PETER. (*Calling to dog off.*) Quiet ! (*Crosses up* L., *puts coat on.*)

MARGUERITE. (*Making herself comfortable.*) Bring her in your arms and don't let her bark.

(PETER *crosses* R. *and takes candle.*) (*Dog howl.*)

PETER. (*He comes back* R.) If I find her, she'll never bark again.

(PETER *puts table centre on head, ties it under his chin, crosses up* C. *to door and exit.*)

(*Pause. A dark landing outside is faintly illuminated by the light of his candle.* MARGUERITE *sits up in bed listening eagerly. Suddenly there comes from the passage the sound of a tin can being hurtled downstairs.* MARGUERITE *jumps out of bed, crosses to door, sees* MRS. SPOKER *and gets back.* MRS. SPOKER, *in night attire, with a dressing-gown, peers into the room.*)

MRS. SPOKER. Was that Mr. Hickett ?

MARGUERITE. It sounded to me more like a can.

MRS. SPOKER. It was a can placed outside the door o' Number One. What is the meaning of this ?

MARGUERITE. My husband has gone to get the dog. She was howling.

MRS. SPOKER. (*Coming into the room* L. C.) What is he going to do with the dog ?

MARGUERITE. Bring her in here, of course.

MRS. SPOKER. I won't allow it ; I've said so once.

MARGUERITE.   She's not going to stay out there and howl all night.

MRS. SPOKER.   I can't hear any noise.

(*Bang of a door from outside.*)

PETER.   (*Off* L.)   Pansy, Pansy, come here, come here, come here!

(*Hens are heard cackling.*   PETER *whistles for* PANSY.)

MRS. SPOKER.   (*Turning, very sternly.*)   What's he up to now?   I've never heard such a thing.   (*Crosses to window. Sees blanket on floor at foot of bed.*)   And what, may I ask, may you be doing with my best blanket and pillows all over the floor?

MARGUERITE.   He was trying to make a bed there.

MRS. SPOKER.   A bed?

MARGUERITE.   Yes, for the dog, you see.

MRS. SPOKER.   Oh, really?   I'll soon settle this.

(*Exit* C.)

(PETER *is heard whistling dog.   Hens cackling in the distance.*)

(MARGUERITE *quickly puts her book on the table and gets out of bed.   She puts on her slippers and hurries to the window.   She puts her head out, but withdraws it again quickly.   She calls through the window.*)

MARGUERITE.   Peter!   Peter!

PETER.   (*Heard off* L.)   Hallo!

MARGUERITE.   Come back!   Mrs. Spoker is on the war-path; come back.

PETER.   I don't know that I *can* come back.   I'm all tied up in pig buckets.

(*Noise of buckets.*)

Oh!

MARGUERITE.   Besides it's pouring with rain.

PETER.   (*Very testily.*)   I know that.

(*Bucket noises.*)

MARGUERITE.   Peter, be careful with those buckets.   The poor pigs won't get their food.

(MARGUERITE *watches* PETER'S *movements through the window.*)

(*Door slam.*)

(*Pause.*)

(MARGUERITE *returns to bed. Takes off her slippers and gets in.* MRS. SPOKER *and* PETER *are heard in altercation outside the door of the room and the landing outside is again lit up.*)

MRS. SPOKER. (*Off.*)   Are you finished ?

PETER. (*Entering* C.)   Yes, I'm finished.

MRS. SPOKER.   Where is the dog ?

PETER.   Run away ; and pray heaven it'll stay away.

MRS. SPOKER.   You keep your prayers for yourself.

PETER.   That's just what I'm doing.

(PETER *enters, and he is very wet.*)

MARGUERITE.   Peter, didn't you go after Pansy when she ran away ?

PETER.   Of course I did.   You've no idea what it's like out there on a night like this with rain like that.

(*Warning : light out.*)

MARGUERITE.   But *imagine* what a wretched night she'll spend.

PETER.   That's the one thing I can imagine.

MARGUERITE. (*Leaning forward and scrutinising him.*)   But, Peter, you're wet.

PETER.   Of course I'm wet.   You can't go dog-hunting in the rain without getting wet.

MARGUERITE.   You must take off those wet clothes at once.

PETER.   I'm not going to take off any clothes in here.

MARGUERITE.   You can't catch pneumonia.

PETER.   I can. (*Crosses* L.)

MARGUERITE.   Go on.   You can't sleep in wet clothes.   I'll put the light out if you're so modest. (*Puts out light on chair by bed.*)   There !

(*Light out.*)

PETER.   You needn't have done that.   I'm only going to take off my coat and shoes.

(*His figure can be dimly seen.   Takes off coat and puts it on horse* L.)

MARGUERITE.   (*After a brief pause.*)   Got your coat off?

PETER.   Not yet—yes.

MARGUERITE.   Hang it over a chair.

PETER.   (*Stubbs his foot suddenly.*)   Oh, my right toe.

MARGUERITE.   Now your shoes.   Got your shoes off?

PETER.   No.   It's very difficult to balance.   I've only one foot on the ground.

MARGUERITE.   Well, take it off.

(PETER *overbalances and clutches at the nearest thing to hand.   He falls and smashes the china jug from the washstand.*)

Good heavens!   What's happened?

PETER.   (*In a desperate voice.*)   Light the light!   Light the light!

(MARGUERITE *strikes a match and lights the lamp.*   PETER *is on his hands and knees, looking very scared.*)

MARGUERITE.   What *have* you done now?

PETER.   I overbalanced and caught hold of the jug.

MARGUERITE.   It made a ghastly row.

PETER.   I think it only sounded loud.

MARGUERITE.   Is the jug broken?

PETER.   Yes, but the handle's all right.   (PETER *picks up the handle of the jug.*)

(MRS. SPOKER *and* GLADYS *talking off.*)

MARGUERITE.   Peter, she's coming.   Stand over there.   (*Indicates* L.)   And pretend to be undressing.

(PETER *makes movement of taking off imaginary trousers.*)

MRS. SPOKER.   What is it, Gladys?

GLADYS.   (*Off.*)   It's cats.

MRS. SPOKER.   Cats, rubbish!

(*Entering, leaving door open, followed by* GLADYS.)

And what are you up to now, may I ask?

MARGUERITE.   My husband was undressing and knocked over a jug.

(GLADYS *in an overcoat over her nightdress and curl papers peers round the door—crosses to* PETER.)

PETER. I'll pay for your jug. Go away, Gladys.

MRS. SPOKER. (*Crosses to front of* GLADYS.) Go you back, Gladys.

(*Exit* GLADYS.)

Unless you're in bed and asleep in five minutes——

MARGUERITE. Yes, yes, he shall be . . . he's always like this.

MRS. SPOKER. Does he break a jug every time he undresses ?

MARGUERITE. I'll pay for it. Or rather he will.

PETER. Oh, go away.

(*A moaning sound from outside.* MRS. SPOKER *turns.*)

MRS. SPOKER. Now you've gone and shook up Number One. I'll go and settle her, and when I come back I shall expect to find you in bed like a respectable gentleman.

(*She goes out, closing the door.*)

PETER. She's gone to settle her. It doesn't matter what happens to me now.

MARGUERITE. Never mind, take those wet clothes off.

PETER. No, I can't undress here.

MARGUERITE. Well, go outside the door.

(PETER *goes out, taking a towel with him from* U. L., *and starts to undress outside.*)

PETER. (*Opens door and looks in.*) We're utterly compromised. (*Closes door—pause.*)

MARGUERITE. Compromised—nonsense ! I tell you what does she matter ?

PETER. (*Looking in.*) It isn't only she. We've tied ourselves in knots all the evening. (*Closes door. Pause—opens door again.*) We're husband and wife in the register book.

MARGUERITE. I know, Peter, but we're all right in the book from which there is no rubbing out.

PETER. (*Peeping in again.*) We're in the same room.

MARGUERITE. I am in the same room, but you seem to be doing a little travelling.

PETER. You can laugh.   You'd laugh while Rome fiddled.
(PETER *closes door.*)

(*Peeping in again.*)   And we've been identified by that parson,
Up Jenkins, or whatever his damn silly name is.   (*Closes door.*)
MARGUERITE.   Hurry up, I tell you—good gracious, what
does it matter ?

> (MRS. SPOKER'S *voice heard off.*)
> (PETER *enters. He has draped himself with a towel, and
> carries his trousers over his arm.   He hides on floor by
> trunk.*)
> (MRS. SPOKER *again heard off.*)   '

MRS. SPOKER.   There's more noise in Number Two.   Come
along, Gladys, I'll soon settle this.

> (MRS. SPOKER *enters with* GLADYS, *pushing door open.*)

MRS. SPOKER.   Where's your husband ?

(*Very startled and coming indignantly towards him.*)
And what are you doing down there ?
PETER.   I'm looking for my collar stud.
MRS. SPOKER.   Come up.

> (MRS. SPOKER *is very shocked when she sees* PETER'S *attire.*)

MARGUERITE.   Bring your trousers here, dear, and press them
under the mattress.
GLADYS. (*Following* PETER.)   'Ere, I'll take 'em for 'ee.
PETER.   Leave them alone.   (*Crosses to bed, raising the mat-
tress.   He puts trousers under mattress.*)   I want to press them
in the creases.
MRS. SPOKER.   Now, Gladys, get you back to bed.
GLADYS.   All ri.'

> (*With a grin at* PETER *as she goes off* C.)

MRS. SPOKER.   Has he got his nightshirt ?
PETER.   Yes ; and go away.
MRS. SPOKER. - Directly I turn my back there's a row.
PETER.   There'll be a bigger one if you don't.
MRS. SPOKER. (*Crosses up* C.)   Why don't you look after
him—— (*At door.*)   I knew how to *manage* my late husband.

PETER.   No wonder he's late.
MRS. SPOKER.   Oh !

(*Exit* MRS. SPOKER *up* C.)

PETER.   That's one to me.

(*Loud knocking off door* R.)

MRS. SPOKER.   (*Off.*) Who and what is that? (*Calls.*)
Gladys !

GLADYS.   (*Off.*) There's someone at the door, Mrs. Spoker.

(*Noise continues until* PETER *goes to door.*)

PETER.   (*At door.*) Stop that row ! How do you expect a
respectable gentleman to sleep. (*Closes door and comes down* C.)

MARGUERITE.   Who was it, Peter ?

PETER.   I don't know ! Someone trying to get a drink or
something. (*Sits on trunk.*)

(*Enter* MRS. BONE *and* MAJOR BONE.)

MRS. BONE.   (D. L. C., *to* MAJOR BONE.)   There !

(PETER *jumps up.   Crosses down* R.)

Look !

MAJOR	MRS. BONE
(R. C.)	(D. L. C.)
MARGUERITE	
PETER	
(D. R.)	

PETER.   This is very unexpected.

MRS. BONE.   (*Crosses* L.)   Not in the least.

PETER.   Oh, well—now you are here, let me introduce you,
Marguerite—Mrs. Bone, my mother-in-law.

(MRS. BONE *turns her back on* MARGUERITE.)

Major Bone, my father-in-ditto.

MAJOR BONE.   (*Affably.*) How de do ? (*Shaking hands with*
MARGUERITE.)

MRS. BONE.   (*To* MAJOR BONE.)   Stop that.

MARGUERITE.   (*Who remains totally unperturbed—to* MRS.
BONE.) Won't you sit down ? I'm afraid the space is rather
limited.

MRS. BONE.   (*To* MARGUERITE.)   So you are the woman ?

MARGUERITE.   Yes, I am the woman and this is the man. (*Indicates* PETER.)   I admit his costume is rather effeminate at the moment.

> (BONE *advances to bed and leans against the bed-rail, looking down at* MARGUERITE.)

MRS. BONE.   I knew very well I should find *you* here.

PETER.   Let me explain.

MRS. BONE.   Explain !   This explains itself.   Here you are in this room with this scarlet woman——

PETER.   What colour ?   (*Crosses* L. *very indignant.*)   How dare you say a thing like that in a room like this !

MRS. BONE.   Barbara will be here in the morning, and I'll see you don't get away till then.

PETER.   But Barbara's at the Bunters'.

MRS. BONE.   Yes, that's what you *think*.

PETER.   Think ?

> (PETER *looks very concerned.*)

MRS. BONE.   So you spend the night here with your alleged wife—she in bed and you in a towel.

PETER.   My trousers are there.

MRS. BONE.   Where ?

> (*They turn towards the bed.*   BONE *blissfully unaware that he is under observation is looking with great interest at* MARGUERITE.)

MARGUERITE.   Under the mattress, if you want them.

MAJOR BONE.   Allow me.   (*He comes eagerly to the bed, places hat on trunk and takes hold of mattress.*)

> (MRS. BONE *stops him.*)

MRS. BONE.   No, you don't.   This room shall stay as it is until Barbara arrives.   That'll be evidence enough.

MARGUERITE.   Evidence of what ?

PETER.   There isn't another room in the house.   They are all completely occupied.

MARGUERITE.   Oh, this is all very restless.   (*Standing up on bed.*)

> (*Enter* MRS. SPOKER C.)

MRS. SPOKER. Out you go, all of you.

MARGUERITE. I cannot go out in the night, in the middle of the rain.

MAJOR BONE. Hear ! Hear !

BONE	MRS. SPOKER	MRS. BONE
(R. C.)	(C.)	(L. C.)
MARGUERITE		PETER
		(D. L.)

MRS. SPOKER. (*To* MAJOR BONE, *brushing him aside*.) I don't know who you are—this is my hotel and out you go, all of you. (*To* MARGUERITE.) You with your lies and deceit and sin.

MRS. BONE. I quite agree.

MRS. SPOKER. (*Brushing* MRS. BONE *aside*.) And don't you interfere.

(PETER *is sitting on chair* D. L. *enjoying the joke*.)

(*To* PETER.) And as for you, out of my house you go.

(PETER *now looks helplessly at* MRS. BONE.)

You—— (*Pause*.) You sheik !

(PETER *looks very annoyed and indignant, repeats* " Sheik," *crosses to step of door, strikes an attitude of injured dignity and goes out*.)

(*As he goes* ALFRED *appears in the doorway in nightshirt and lighted candlestick in hand, looking off* R.)

CURTAIN

ACT III

SCENE: *The Parlour.*
TIME: *Morning.*

(PETER, BONE, MARGUERITE *and* MRS. BONE *all discovered asleep in various places.* MARGUERITE *and* MRS. BONE *on bench.* MRS. BONE *has* MAJOR BONE'S *overcoat over her.* MAJOR BONE *on chair* R. *of table, and* PETER *on the floor, resting his head against front leg of table* L. *All dressed as at end of* ACT II.)

(*Enter down* L. GLADYS *with hot-water can. She is followed by* ALFRED.)

ALFRED. Gladys!
GLADYS. What?
ALFRED. (*To* GLADYS.) Walking with a pig-lad won't never win success.

(GLADYS *merely snorts and exit* R.)
(PETER *opens his eyes and in rising rubs his neck and shoulder, which are obviously stiff by lying in a draught. He crosses to bar.*)

PETER. Here, Alfred!
ALFRED. Sur?
PETER. Sh! Listen! Was that Gladys went through?
ALFRED. Aye, sur.
PETER. Well, tell her to try and get into that bedroom somehow and get my trousers. They're in the bed.
ALFRED. On the bed?
PETER. *In* the bed.
ALFRED. What, under the clothes?
PETER. Yes. Under the mattress.
ALFRED. Under the mattress? How come they to have got corrt there, sur?
PETER. They didn't get corrt. Tell Gladys. She knows. Oh, and Alfred?
ALFRED. Aye, sur.

PETER.   Get me a beer.

ALFRED.   A beer, sur ?

MAJOR BONE.   (R. C., *opening his eyes.*)   What's that ?

PETER   Sh !   (*To* ALFRED.)   Two beers !

ALFRED.   Aye, sur.   Which first ?   The trousers or the beers ?

MAJOR BONE.   The beers.

ALFRED.   Aye, sur.

(*Exit into bar.*)

PETER.   (*Crosses to* R. *above table, glances at* MRS. BONE.)
I say, Bone !   (*Takes* BONE *by* R. *arm, crosses* L. C. *by front of
table.*)

MAJOR BONE.   Yes, my boy ?

PETER.   Where did mother put the key of that room ?

MAJOR BONE.   In the tail pocket of her skirt.   (L. *of table.*)

PETER.   I suppose you wouldn't care to try and get it ?

MAJOR BONE.   H'm !   (*Looking at seat* R.)   Pretty ticklish
job.

PETER.   Oh, of course, if she's ticklish it's hopeless.

MAJOR BONE.   Anyhow, don't let's risk waking her up until
we've had the beers.   There are one or two devilish awkward
points about this affair, you know.

PETER.   There shouldn't be (*moving to* R. *end of table, front of
it, looking at* MARGUERITE), because Mrs. Hickett is even more
virtuous than she is beautiful.

MARGUERITE.   (*Opening her eyes quickly.*)   Don't be rude.

MAJOR BONE.   Hallo !   Good morning.   (*Leaning on left end
table facing* R.)

MARGUERITE.   'Morning.   You ought to know better than
to make remarks about a lady when she is asleep.   Because she
never is.

MRS. BONE.   (*Opening her eyes, speaking pointedly to* BONE.)
Never.

PETER.   (*Crossing to* MRS. BONE, *to her.*)   Well, if you're
awake, you'd better give me the key of the room.

MRS. BONE.   You will stay as you are till Barbara comes.

(PETER *crosses down* L.)

MARGUERITE.   (*Shivering.*)   Boo !   Well, I hope Barbara is better at catching trains than her husband, or there will be two bedridden ladies in this hotel.

MAJOR BONE. Quite right—this lady must have her clothes.

PETER. Yes, and the same remark applies to this gentleman and his trousers.

MARGUERITE. (*Rises and crosses to above chair* R. C.) If this goes on, and the natives come in for their morning beer, what will they say to see me standing here like this ?

MRS. BONE. H'mph !

MARGUERITE. H'mph, yes. That is just what they *will* say. And do you think I am going to stand here and be h'mphed at by Maiden Blotton ?

> (MRS. BONE *puts* BONE'S *overcoat over back of bench and sits on bench.*)

MAJOR BONE. (*To* PETER.) I say, that reminds me. What about those two beers ?

PETER. That's all right. I'll go and have them.

> (PETER *goes into bar.*)

MAJOR BONE. That will be nice for me. (*To* MRS. BONE.) Look here, Constance, I entirely agree with Mrs. Hitchcock. It's a bit too thick.

MARGUERITE. No, it's a bit too thin. (*Is above chair* R. C. *to* BONE.) Do you know that pretty little picture " September Morn " ?

MAJOR BONE. Rather !

MARGUERITE. The poor little girl with no clothes on, standing shivering in the cold pond ?

MAJOR BONE. Yes. But why she wanted to go paddling dressed like that I'm blowed if I can say.

MARGUERITE. Now that I know how cold she felt, *I* can't say either.

MAJOR BONE. And there was a stork——

MRS. BONE. George !

MAJOR BONE. (*Turning from* MARGUERITE.) Where's Peter gone, I wonder ? (*He is crossing to bar when*—

> (CHAUFFEUR *enters at front door.*)

E

CHAUFFEUR. (*Up* C.) Begging your pardon, but 'ow much longer——? (*Seeing* MARGUERITE.) Oh, my lord!

MARGUERITE. There you are! There's the first! (*Crosses and sits* R. C.)

MAJOR BONE. It's all right. It's the gentleman who's driving our car.

CHAUFFEUR. Driving it? It's the gent. who wants to. I've bin sleeping in it. What's the game?

MRS. BONE. Wait for further orders.

CHAUFFEUR. All very well. I——

MAJOR BONE. (*Going to him* L. C.) Now don't argue—you come in here with me.

CHAUFFEUR. Yes, guv'nor, but listen now——

(BONE *and* CHAUFFEUR *argue at back.*)

(*Enter* PETER *and* MRS. SPOKER *up* L. PETER *close on her heels crosses* D. R.)

MRS. SPOKER. I will not 'ave this person in my 'otel. Give him his trousers at once.

(MARGUERITE *rises and goes to* PETER, R.)

MRS. BONE. He will wait here for his wife.

MRS. SPOKER. He can wait in the trousers. And that person dressed. I will not 'ave my parlour looking like a swimming bath.

(MARGUERITE *and* PETER *go up stage.*)

(*Enter* ALFRED L. *with beers.*)

MRS. BONE. (*Going to* L. *of table.*) I will not give up the key.

MRS. SPOKER. (R. *of table.*) You will!

MRS. BONE. I will not!

MRS. SPOKER. This is my 'otel——

MRS. BONE. Hotel—humph!

MRS. SPOKER. And I keep my own keys.

(ALFRED *places beer-mug in front of each of them.*)

MRS. BONE. I do not intend to give up the key. I depend on it for my evidence.

MRS. SPOKER. I will not have it.

MARGUERITE. I demand to get my clothes. (*Crosses* R. C.)

MRS. SPOKER. Yes, and I'll see that you do.

CHAUFFEUR. Look here, I can't wait.
MRS. BONE. Don't you dare to speak to me !
MARGUERITE. I'm as cold as ice.

(PETER *obtains his beer from table* C. MAJOR BONE *also obtains beer.*)

MRS. SPOKER. You wait till you get to the next world. (*Crosses* R.)
CHAUFFEUR. I've been here all night ; I ain't going to stay here all day.
MRS. BONE. Most men try to get paid for doing nothing.
CHAUFFEUR. What I wants to know is, how much longer have I got to wait ?
MRS. BONE. George ! Take this blot of a man away.
MAJOR BONE. You come in here with me.

(*Takes* CHAUFFEUR *into bar.*)

I'll look after you.
MRS. BONE. I must have my evidence.
MRS. SPOKER. (*Crosses* L., *to* MRS. BONE.) You've proof enough. I saw 'em myself, and there's the Visitors' Book.

(*Crosses to sideboard.*)

(*Coming back with book.*) Here it is.
MRS. BONE. Give it to me—let me see it.

(MRS. SPOKER *places Visitors' Book on table. The other three all collect over it.*)

PETER. Now, now, girls, please !
MRS. BONE. (*Reading an entry scornfully, with sarcasm.*) " Mr. and Mrs. Love. Room Number Two."
MRS. SPOKER. That ain't them.
MARGUERITE. That ain't us.
MRS. BONE. (*Reading.*) " Remarks—most comfortable."
PETER. That *certainly* isn't us ! What have these Loves been used to ? (*Crosses* R.)
MRS. SPOKER. This is what applies to them. (*Pointing to register.*) " Mr. 'Ickett, M.P., and Mrs. 'Ickett. Room Number Two."
PETER. Remarks ? Give me a page and a pen !

MARGUERITE. I should put " one bed and one board." (*Sits* R. C.)

PETER. And three blasts.

MRS. BONE. Very well. (*Closing book.*) This book will suffice. I'll take charge of it till my daughter comes. You may take your key. (*Hands key to* MRS. SPOKER.)

MARGUERITE. Then I'm to go and dress?

MRS. SPOKER. You're to dress and go!

(MARGUERITE *crosses* R.)

(*Gives* MARGUERITE *key.*) And when she's finished (*to* PETER) you can get your trousers.

PETER. What about breakfast?

MRS. SPOKER. You'll get no breakfast from me!

PETER. Oh, come now—bed and breakfast.

MRS. BONE. I shall require some breakfast. (*Up* L.C.)

PETER. Certainly. (*To* MARGUERITE.) Tea or coffee, Mrs. Hickett? (*To fireplace.*)

MARGUERITE. Strong coffee. (*To* MRS. SPOKER.)

PETER. And I'll have two boiled eggs.

MARGUERITE. Hard or soft? (R. C.)

PETER. Medium.

MARGUERITE. (*To* MRS. SPOKER.) You hear? Two strong coffees and four sticky eggs!

(*Exit* MARGUERITE R.)

MRS. SPOKER. You won't get a bite out of me!

PETER. I don't want one. I'm a vegetarian.

(*Exit* MRS. SPOKER D. L.)

MRS. BONE. (*Going after* MARGUERITE, *at door* U. R.) I don't want to let that woman out of my sight.

(*Exit* MRS. BONE R.)

PETER. I can't say the same about you! (*Closes door* R.)

(MAJOR BONE *looks out of bar, sees her go, and comes out, down* L. C.)

PETER. (*Crosses to* BONE, *below table.*) I say, look here, Bone, old boy, I'm in an awful fix. Barbara will be here at any moment—be a sport and help me.

MAJOR BONE. All very well—but it's no easy matter. This lady friend of yours is foreign and very attractive, and the two together are generally looked upon as a foregone conclusion.

PETER. Still, by the time Barbara comes, I shall be in my trousers. At least, I hope so. I can't stand and make speeches in a towel. I'm not a Roman Senator.

MAJOR BONE. You needn't worry about your towel. If you are going to tell Barbara that you stayed here last night in that delightful creature's room only to keep away the mice, it won't make the slightest difference whether you are wearing a towel or a suit of chain armour.

PETER. (*Crosses* D. R.) But that's not the point. The point is—what am I going to tell her?

MAJOR BONE. Tell her the truth.

PETER. Impossible. She wouldn't believe it. She oughtn't to doubt me. It isn't as if I were you!

MAJOR BONE. What d'you mean?

PETER. I mean my record's pure.

MAJOR BONE. Well, isn't mine? I like that, when I'm trying to help you, you start abusing me! That's not the way to get assistance.

PETER. I don't mean that. What am I to tell her? You ought to know. Besides, really you're an expert.

MAJOR BONE. (*Pleased.*) Do you really think so? That's very nice of you. I oughtn't to help you. It isn't playing the game, you know—but there you are. Well, I'm a man of the world, and you're a very decent boy, and so I don't see why you shouldn't have the benefit of my experience. Now I'll tell you. When Barbara arrives, when she comes in this door—I presume that's where she'll come in—you stand there looking bewildered and ill-used.

PETER. That's easy.

MAJOR BONE. Now, the first thing she'll say will be, " Peter ! What is this I hear ? "

PETER. " What is this I hear ? "

MAJOR BONE. Yes, they always say that.

PETER. Do they? I didn't know.

MAJOR BONE. Yes, you can lay odds on that. And you turn

rouud and say, "It's nothing, darling. Surely you know me better than that?"

PETER. Better than what?

MAJOR BONE. Better than what?

PETER. Better than what?

MAJOR BONE. What what? Oh, better than what? Why, better than what she has heard. Then *I'll* step into the breach——

PETER. Out of the bar.

MAJOR BONE. Thank you very much—and say to her, " Oh, believe me, Barbara, you're utterly wrong." And you must tell her the tale.

PETER. What tale?

MAJOR BONE. The tale of the old iron pot.

PETER. Old iron pot?

MAJOR BONE. That's another way of saying " Spin her the yarn." This is a good one. Tell her that Hitchcock stayed here with his wife——

PETER. Who?

MAJOR BONE. Hitchcock.

PETER. *Hickett.*

MAJOR BONE. Hickett—is that the name? Good Lor'! I've been calling her Mrs. Hitchcock. The husband stayed here with the wife and you went on elsewhere.

PETER. By Jove, Bone, that's fine! Shall we try? You be Barbara!

MAJOR BONE. It's rather difficult—but I'll have a shot at it.

(PETER *crosses*, BONE U. L. *to* C.)

PETER. (D. R.) Bewildered and——

MAJOR BONE. Ill-used.

PETER. I'm ready. (*Strikes attitude.*)

(MAJOR BONE *knocks.*)

What's that——?

MAJOR BONE. That's in case she knocks. (*Coming down* R. C.)

PETER. Barbara, darling!

MAJOR BONE. Peter! What is *this* I *hear*?

PETER. It's nothing, darling. Surely you know me better than that! (*Places hands on* BONE'S *shoulders.*)

MAJOR BONE. Good! (*Places hands on* PETER'S *shoulders as he says this and they bob together.*) Then she'll say, " You've been false to me." (*Throwing* PETER *off.*)

PETER. What? (*Poses with arms outspread.*)

MAJOR BONE. That's good—hold that! Now I'll be me. (*Crosses* L. C. *to* L. *corner of table, his left hand supporting him.*) Oh! Believe me, Barbara, you are utterly wrong! (*His hand slips from table and he overbalances slightly.*) Then you go on with the tale.

PETER. And you go back to the bar.

MAJOR BONE. Thanks very much. (L. C., *front of table.*) You see, the husband stayed here with the wife, and you pushed on and stayed elsewhere.

PETER. (R. C., *front of table.*) By Jove, Bone, that's fine! Then there's the Visitors' Book. Mr. and Mrs. Hickett not in my handwriting—all cut and dried.

MAJOR BONE. 'Course—it can't go wrong.

PETER. Then I can rely on you?

MAJOR BONE. Absolutely.

PETER. Thank you, Bone, thank you——

(*They shake hands.*)

MAJOR BONE. Don't thank me, my boy. I hope one of these days you'll be able to do as much for me.

(PETER *crosses up to door* R.)

Peter, they're wonderful things, wives.

PETER. Oh, wonderful! I'm delighted you've got yours!

(*Exit* PETER R.)

MAJOR BONE. He's a very good boy, with a very promising future. (D. L. *of table.*)

(*Enter* MRS. SPOKER. MAJOR BONE *is just going back into bar, gets in her way, they try to pass each other, but both move the same way.*)

I'm afraid you'll have to excuse me, I'm not very good at the Schottische! (*Exit* BONE *into bar.*)

(SLOLEY-JONES *enters at front door.*)

SLOLEY-J. Good morning, Mrs. Spoker.

(MRS. SPOKER *sees him and speaks indignantly.*)
MRS. SPOKER. We don't want you here. (*Crosses* D. L.)
I am not yet open to the public.
SLOLEY-J. Righto! Righto! I'm only just giving myself
an early morning test. (*Crosses above table* C. *and takes off
gloves.*)
MRS. SPOKER. Quite enough trouble without you. (*Crosses
*L. *with back to audience.*)
SLOLEY-J. Trouble?
MRS. SPOKER. (*At bar door.*) Alfred!
(ALFRED *enters from bar.*)
ALFRED. Aye, Mrs. Spoker?
MRS. SPOKER. Come you here. I am going to make the tea.
When those two persons come down from dressing, make sure
they don't go without they pay.
ALFRED. Aye, Mrs. Spoker.
(*Exit* MRS. SPOKER *down* L.)
SLOLEY-J. What two persons? (*Crosses* L. C.) Surely she
doesn't mean the Hicketts?
ALFRED. Aye, there's trouble. In and out of his bed all
night 'e were. 'E lost his dog; he lost his trousers, he grubbled
up his room and he burst his jug.
SLOLEY-J. Lost his dog? How did he come to lose his dog?
(GLADYS *enters* R.)
ALFRED. It happened loike this—the dog were in the stables—
and it were howling so much that he thought——
(*He sees* GLADYS *as she crosses* L., *and without another
word he follows her fascinated out down* L. *with a broad
grin.*)
(*At the same moment* NOONY *enters cautiously at front door,
carrying* PANSY.)
NOONY. Here! Mister! (*Coming down* L. C.) Oh, good
day to 'e, parson. (*Taking off hat.*)
SLOLEY-J. (*Up* L.) Hallo, by Christopher! You've found
the dog! (*Putting gloves in his left-hand pocket.*)
NOONY. Be this the one that belong to the lady?
SLOLEY-J. Yes! Splendid! Give it to me.

NOONY. No, sur. Finding be delivering. (*Inside* U. L.)

SLOLEY-J. Well, then, you'd better stay in here with it.

NOONY. Be Mrs. Spoker in ?

SLOLEY-J. Yes, of course.

NOONY. Then I reckon I'll bide in the road ! (*He turns as if to go out* U. C.)

(HICKETT, *a middle-aged man, wearing lounge suit and overcoat and cap in his hand, enters front door* U. C., *running.*)

HICKETT. Ah, there you are, my man ! Excuse me, what dog's that ?

NOONY. I found her down along.

HICKETT. Where did you get that dog ? Let me see it.

NOONY. She belong in here—she belong in here.

HICKETT. I want to see its collar.

NOONY. (*Coming down a little.*) She belong in here.

(HICKETT *examines* PANSY *and her collar. Then looks up, quite convinced.*)

HICKETT. Yes, of course, I knew it—I'd recognise that dog anywhere. How the devil did it come here ?

SLOLEY-J. Excuse me, sir ; I can tell you all about the dog.

NOONY. She belong to a lady.

HICKETT. I know quite well who it belongs to.

SLOLEY-J. He's quite right, quite. It belongs to a man and his wife who are staying here for the night on their way to Lady Bunter's at Rushcombe.

(NOONY *attempts to go.*)

HICKETT. Lady Bunter's is where I'm going myself. This is Mrs. Hickett's dog.

SLOLEY-J. That's right. Mr. and Mrs. Hickett had a breakdown in their car and had to stay here.

HICKETT. Mr. and Mrs. Hickett ?

SLOLEY-J. Yes. They're here now. I know all about it.

HICKETT. But Mrs. Hickett went by train to Rushcombe yesterday afternoon.

SLOLEY-J. You'll excuse me, but Mrs. Hickett is still upstairs with her husband. (*Crosses* D. L.)

HICKETT. (*After a moment's bewildered thought, turning on* NOONY.) Here, my man, here's half-a-crown for you, now give me that dog. (*Taking* PANSY.)

NOONY. I thank you, sir, you can have her—I thank you. (*Takes the coin and creeps out up* C., *crossing in front of* HICKETT.)

HICKETT. (*Crossing down* L. C. *to* JONES, *in more practical tones.*) You're under some delusion, sir. Whatever has happened to Mrs. Hickett, I can tell you on very good authority that her husband spent last night in Bristol on his way from London.

SLOLEY-J. Indeed he didn't, if you'll pardon me. He spent last night getting in and out of bed after this dog, poor fellow. From all accounts he and Mrs. Hickett had a very rough time !

HICKETT But——

SLOLEY-J. I saw them here myself last night.

HICKETT. Oh, then *you know* Mr. Hickett ?

SLOLEY-J. Yes, I knew his wife before. She introduced me to him. He's Hickett the M.P., you know. I was agreeably surprised—a very decent fellow. I'd always been told that the man was a bit of an ass !

HICKETT. Indeed ! (*With meaning.*) I think I'll wait here and see. (*Crossing* R.)

SLOLEY-J. Righto ! You might be very useful to them. (*He moves up as though to go.*)

HICKETT. By the way, as you go, you might be kind enough to put the dog in my car.

SLOLEY-J. In your car ?

HICKETT. Yes, I'll see that Mrs. Hickett gets it. It's a two-seater. (*Crosses* U. L.)

SLOLEY-J. (*Taking* PANSY.) With pleasure. (*To* PANSY.) Come along then, naughty to run away from kind mistress ! (*Going.*) Oh dear, oh dear, it spat on my chin !

(*Exit.*)

(HICKETT *stands spellbound up stage.*)
(MRS. SPOKER *enters down* L. *and comes and puts tablecloth on table. When she speaks she barely notices him.*)

HICKETT. Oh, excuse me, please——

MRS. SPOKER. I am completely occupied.

(*She goes out again down* L.)
(MAJOR BONE *puts his head out from bar.*)
MAJOR BONE.   Barman !
HICKETT.   Oh, excuse me, sir——
MAJOR BONE.   I beg your pardon.
HICKETT.   I'm just looking for a couple——
MAJOR BONE.   Yes, so am I, but I can't find the barman !
(*Exit into bar.*)
(*Enter* MRS. BONE *and* PETER R. PETER *is now fully clad.*
MRS. BONE *still holds the Visitors' Book. During the
next few lines* PETER *takes much interest in the proceed-
ings without suspecting in the least who* HICKETT *is.*)
(PETER *comes down first*—R.)
HICKETT.   Oh, are you the manageress ?   (*Crosses* R. C.)
(PETER *laughs and crosses to fireplace* D. R.)
MRS. BONE.   Manageress !   (*Coming down* R. C.)
HICKETT.   Oh, I beg your pardon.   I thought that looked like
the register.
MRS. BONE.   So it is.   Why ?
HICKETT.   Ah !   May I see it, please ?
MRS. BONE.   Certainly not !
HICKETT.   But I wish to see it.
MRS. BONE.   Who are you ?
HICKETT.   I have every right to see it, madam.
PETER.   (*Taking book from* MRS. BONE *and giving it to* HICKETT.)
Certainly.   Give the gentleman the book.   (*Crossing* L., *takes
ink bottle from dresser* L., *puts it on table* C.)   Where are the pens,
the ink and the blotting-paper ?   (*Bus.*)
HICKETT.   (*After examining book keenly, takes stock of* PETER.)
Did you stay at this hotel last night ?
PETER.   Yes—in and out.
HICKETT.   Is this your name ?
PETER.   (*Up to above table—looks at book.*)   Yes, why
shouldn't it be ?
HICKETT.   Because it's mine !
(MRS. BONE *is obviously pleased.*)
PETER.   Oh, then you'd better have it.

HICKETT. Quite by chance I recognised my wife's dog and stopped here. Will you explain?

MRS. BONE. I can do that.

PETER. No, no, I'll see Marguerite.

HICKETT. Marguerite!

PETER. My wife—your wife—our wife——

HICKETT. Who the devil are you?

PETER. I don't know now. I used to be a nice little fellow. I've gone off.

MRS. BONE. He spent the night in her room. (*Crosses* C.)

HICKETT. Is this true?

PETER. Well, yes, in a way. (*Crosses* D. L.)

HICKETT. What the devil d'you mean, sir? (*Crosses to* PETER.) How can you spend the night in a lady's room in a way.

PETER. Oh, you can—believe me.

HICKETT. What excuse have you got?

PETER. The landlady wouldn't take us in unless we were married. So we were married.

HICKETT. Married?

PETER. Well, you know what I mean. We *said* we were.

HICKETT. Why wouldn't the landlady take you in unmarried?

PETER. Because she's a sort of Prussian Baptist.

HICKETT. That's not good enough. (*Crosses* R.)

(PETER *follows* HICKETT R. MRS. BONE *follows* C.)

Now look here, sir. I've always had the best reasons to regard my wife as a sweet and innocent woman.

(*Enter* BONE *from the bar.*)

MAJOR BONE. (*Blundering in from bar, coming down* L. C.) Then believe me—you're utterly wrong!

PETER. (*Crosses* L. C.) Pull yourself together! This is something entirely different!

MAJOR BONE. (*Staring at* HICKETT.) Good lord! Have I dropped a brick!

PETER. No. You've pushed over the whole building.

MAJOR BONE. Oh, I'm frightfully sorry! (*Returns to bar.*)

PETER. (*Crosses* R.) What he really means is—if you think your wife is capable of doing anything wrong——

HICKETT. Wrong? My wife? I should be sorry for the person who dared say so !

MRS. BONE. (*Staggered.*) You'd be sorry?

HICKETT. My wife is the most innocent woman in England.

MRS. BONE. But I tell you I caught them red-handed.

PETER. Oh ! That is a false-*hood*.

HICKETT. (*To* PETER.) Where is my wife now ?

PETER. Getting up.

HICKETT. How do *you* know ?

PETER. She said " I'm going to get up." (*Crosses* U. C.)

HICKETT. (*Impatiently, crosses up* R. C.) Now look here, sir. I'm going to learn the truth about this.

(*This line takes* HICKETT *over* R. C. *and*—MARGUERITE *opens the door and confronts him with a cry of surprise.*)

MARGUERITE. Claude, darling !

HICKETT. (*In fervent anxiety.*) Marguerite !

MARGUERITE. How on earth did you get here ?

HICKETT. My angel ! What has been happening to you !

PETER. Marguerite ! I'm so glad you've arrived—do take him away and explain.

MARGUERITE. Yes, darling. Come with me, and I'll make it all clear to you.

HICKETT. But the *fact remains*—— (*With emphasis.*)

MARGUERITE. No, no, it doesn't, dear.

PETER. No, no, it doesn't, dear. (*To* MRS. BONE.)

HICKETT. Well, I'll hear what you have to say.

MARGUERITE. Well, come with me.

(HICKETT *goes up with* MARGUERITE *and out at porch.*)

MRS. BONE. (C., *to* PETER.) You needn't think you've scored. I'll bring proof.

(GLADYS *enters* L. *with broom and dustpan.* ALFRED *follows her.*)

(*Turns to* GLADYS, *to her.*) Where is the landlady ?

GLADYS. (*Crossing—in front of* PETER.) Gone to get some milk.

MRS. BONE.   Where from?

GLADYS.   From the cauw.

(*Exit* GLADYS R.)

MRS. BONE.   (*To* ALFRED, *who is going to bar.*)   Here, you!
Where is the cow?

ALFRED.   Being milked.

MRS. BONE.   But *where's* the cow being milked?

ALFRED.   (*At bar door.*)   Well, you knows where to milk a
cow, don't 'ee?

(*Exit* ALFRED *into bar.*)

(PETER R. C.   MRS. BONE *looks round.*)

(MARGUERITE *and* HICKETT *appear at porch.*)

MRS. BONE.   (*Going* L.)   I'll find her.   (*Glancing back at*
MARGUERITE.)   His angel!   Hoo!

(PETER *crosses up* L. *round table, meets* MARGUERITE.)

(*Exit* MRS. BONE *down* L.)

(MARGUERITE *and* HICKETT *cross* D. R.)

HICKETT.   Now look here, sir, don't interrupt.

PETER.   (R. C.)   I'm delighted, Mr. Hickett, to say you're an
ideal husband.

(BONE *enters from bar.*)

MARGUERITE.   It's easy to be an ideal husband to a wife like
me!

PETER.   Is it?   I didn't find it at all easy.

HICKETT.   What's that?   (*Crosses* R. C. *to* PETER.)

PETER.   I didn't mean that.   (*Falling back on* BONE *for
support.*)

MAJOR BONE.   (L. C.)   All right, I'm here.   Leave this to me,
my boy.   I know what I'm going to say.

PETER.   Well, don't say it!   (*He whispers to* BONE.)   This is
Hickett!

MAJOR BONE.   Oh, is this the husband?

HICKETT.   Yes, it *is* the husband!

MAJOR BONE.   Oh, that's very awkward.

HICKETT.   (*To* MARGUERITE.)   As regards you, I'm prompted
to believe what you tell me——

MARGUERITE   HICKETT   PETER   BONE

MARGUERITE. Well, you always have so far.
HICKETT. Yes. (*Crosses to* PETER L. C., *pulls him round.*)
It's you.
PETER. Who, me?
HICKETT. Now look here, sir, I want to trust my wife. I've
always thought her above suspicion. That's been my greatest
pride and joy.
PETER. Many happy returns of the day!
HICKETT. (*To* PETER, *with contempt.*) But you tell me you
couldn't sleep anywhere else.
PETER. I tell you I couldn't sleep anywhere at all!
HICKETT. Oh, rot! That's past belief. I won't put up with
it.
PETER. Put up with it! I wish you'd had to put up with it.
If that's the sort of night you spend with your wife, you ought
to be grateful to me.
HICKETT. Grateful to you?
PETER. Yes, for spending one for you.
HICKETT. Now look here! (*He shakes his fist in* PETER'S
face.)

(MAJOR BONE *gets between* PETER *and* HICKETT. BONE
turns to PETER, *who is holding up his right hand.*)

MAJOR BONE. Put it down, put it down! Come, come, none
of that! No fighting here. You listen to me for a moment. I
am a man of the world, and I happen to be the father of this man's
wife's daughter.

(*General movement.* MARGUERITE *and* HICKETT *go up
stage* R., *and come down again.* PETER *crosses to dresser
and rattles cups, then comes over to* BONE, *kneels on
table and whispers in his ear.*)

HICKETT. (*To* PETER.) Is this your father-in-law?
PETER. I'm afraid it is.
HICKETT. Then you have a wife?
PETER. Yes. I've got a little wife.
MARGUERITE. She'll be here soon, perhaps she'll believe
what you say.

PETER. Yes. I shall say what she believes. And get her away quickly.

HICKETT. (*To* PETER.) Oh, so I'm to sit and endorse lies? (*Crosses* L. C., *turning away angrily.*)

MARGUERITE. (*Crosses to* HICKETT, *to him.*) Claude! Listen!

HICKETT. Quiet, please!

MARGUERITE. But listen. His wife's mother still accuses me. He and I are still in the same bed——

(PETER *and* HICKETT *look at* MARGUERITE.)

PETER. What?

MARGUERITE. —boat.

PETER. Yes, and if her mother gets hold of my wife first the boat will sink.

MAJOR BONE. Hear, hear!

PETER. Quiet!

HICKETT. But you haven't finished with *me* yet. *I've* got to decide too.

MARGUERITE. Let me do that for you, as usual.

HICKETT. Oh, leave me alone. I want to think. (*Goes up* L. *to* C.)

PETER. Yes, let him think.

MARGUERITE. But he thinks the worst.

HICKETT. (*Quickly.*) No, I haven't said that.

MARGUERITE. Then what *do* you think? (*Crosses to* HICKETT.)

PETER. He's trying to think what to think.

HICKETT. I know what I think of *you.*

(*He walks off, annoyed.*)
(MARGUERITE *is following,* PETER *stops her, brings her down* L. C.)

MARGUERITE. I want to speak to Claude.

PETER. Let him get some fresh air. We've got Barbara fixed. (*To* BONE.) Haven't we, Bone?

MAJOR BONE. Well, we *had* before he turned up.

(MARGUERITE *makes movement towards 'door, but* PETER *holds her back.*)

PETER. When Barbara comes she's sure to say—" What is this I hear ? " and I'll say, " It's nothing, darling. Surely you know me better than that ! "   Then Bone will breeze in from the bar——

MAJOR BONE. Thanks very much.

PETER. And say, " Believe me, Barbara, you're utterly wrong."

MARGUERITE. And so you think that is going to " fix " Barbara ?

PETER. No. Then I shall explain.

MARGUERITE. What are you going to say ?

PETER. Never mind that now. So long as you back me up when the time comes.

(*Car heard off.*)

MAJOR BONE. Listen ! (*Crosses up* R. C.) I think the time's come. Don't you hear ?

MARGUERITE. What ?

MAJOR BONE. It sounds like Carbara in a bar. Barbara in a car. (*Crosses up stage and looks out of door* C.) Yes, it is !

PETER. Go on, Bone, old boy—you go back in the bar.

MAJOR BONE. Now don't forget. (*Up stage* L.) She'll say, " Peter, what is this I hear ? "—and you say——

MARGUERITE. " It's nothing, darling. Surely you know me better than that."

MAJOR BONE. Good. " Believe me, Barbara, you're utterly wrong——" Yes.

(BONE *goes into bar.*)

PETER. (*Crosses* D. R.) One moment—my attitude—— (*Poses.*) Bewildered and ill-used.

MARGUERITE. No, no. Nonchalant.

PETER. Oh, nonchalong ? (*Poses—mutters.*) " What is this I hear ? "   " It's nothing, darling. Surely you know me better than that ! "

(*Enter* BARBARA C.)

Barbara, darling !

BARBARA. Peter, what is this—— ?

PETER. Well—— ? Go on—what is this you what ?

BARBARA. Well, what is this I—find ?

F

PETER. (*Muddled.*) You don't hear anything? It's nothing, darling. Surely you don't know me as well as all that.

(MARGUERITE L. *of table.*)

BARBARA. Peter! What's happened!

PETER. Nothing, darling. Do I look as if anything has happened?

BARBARA. Think of what's happened to me!

PETER. Yes, I know. All my carelessness—and Mrs. Hickett's—Mrs. Hickett, my wife.

(MARGUERITE *rises.*)

BARBARA. Oh, indeed! (*Crosses* L. C.)

MARGUERITE. Don't be alarmed. We're only so pleased you've come.

PETER. Yes. Lucky I was back in time to meet you.

BARBARA. Back? Haven't you stayed here, then?

PETER. No thanks, no fear. No, I'll tell you. Mrs. Hickett and I met on the platform. She was going to the Bunters too.

MARGUERITE. (*Crosses* L. C.) We talked, you see, and missed the train.

PETER. (*To* MARGUERITE *aside.*) Yes, all right, I'll tell you when I want you to recite. (*To* BARBARA.) So we took a car after you, the car exploded and we came here.

BARBARA. Yes, I heard that.

PETER. Oh, you heard that—well now hear this: and we hadn't been here long when in came Mr. Hickett. (*To* MARGUERITE.) Didn't he?

MARGUERITE. Certainly.

PETER. He certainly did. He was going to the Bunters too.

MARGUERITE. Yes, he heard about us——

PETER. —and came in his two-seater. So he stayed here with Mrs. Hickett, and I pushed on where—else—elsewhere.

BARBARA. To the Bunters?

PETER. No. To the next town.

BARBARA. Why didn't you stay here?

MARGUERITE. There are only two rooms here.

PETER. Yes. The Hicketts had Number Two—very nice room, I believe.

BARBARA. I see. But why didn't you stay in Number One?
MARGUERITE. There's an old lady in bed there.
BARBARA. (*With a smile.*) Oh!
PETER. Yes, and she wanted to be alone—so I went on.
Rang up the Bunters. Heard you weren't there, and came back
here this morning.
BARBARA. Oh, Peter! Then I need never have had any
doubt or anxiety. (*Embracing him.*)
    (BONE *enters from bar.*)
BONE. (*Crosses* D. L.) Oh, believe me, Barbara; you're
utterly wrong!
PETER. (*Crossing to him.*) Well meant, but a bad spot.
MAJOR BONE. (*Subsiding.*) What? Have I done it again?
BARBARA. Father! Are you here?
MAJOR BONE. Yes. I think so. Yes, I'm here.
BARBARA. Is mother here?
MAJOR BONE.⎫ (*Together.*) ⎧No!
PETER.   ⎭   ⎩Yes!
    (*Then correcting themselves.*)
MAJOR BONE.⎫ (*Together.*) ⎧Yes!
PETER.   ⎭   ⎩No!
BARBARA. Peter, where is mother?
PETER. Mother! (*To* BONE.) You know mother, don't
you? Mother's gone to see a little cow.
BARBARA. A little cow? Why?
MARGUERITE. Oh yes, the most famous little cow. The
champion cow of Somerset.
PETER. A long distance cow.
BARBARA. Yes, tell me. (*Moves* L. *to* PETER.) How did you
get to the next town last night?
PETER. What?
MARGUERITE. He borrowed my husband's two-seater. (*Sits
down* R. *of table.*)
MAJOR BONE. Good, good! (*Moves up* L. *to* C., *behind
table.*)
PETER. Yes, splendid little car. It's out there now, with
tyres all round it.

BARBARA. I wish I'd known all this before. What was the name of this town?

PETER. Which town?

BARBARA. The town you stayed at.

PETER · What?

MARGUERITE. Witchtown, wasn't it?

PETER. Yes, I was just telling my wife, Mrs. Hickett. Witchtown, darling. They used to burn witches there, you know.

BARBARA. Did you stay at an hotel?

PETER. Yes—I stayed at the—local—hotel.

BARBARA. What was it called?

PETER. No, no, you mean what name was it? It gives me more time to think. The—er—what? Hotel? An old English name. The—er—Cow and Litter.

BARBARA. The Cow and Litter! (*Laughs in ridicule.*)

(BONE *looks up, anticipating trouble.*)

PETER. Yes. (*Laughs.*)

BARBARA. Nonsense. Cows don't have litters!

(PETER *laughs.*)

MAJOR BONE. Of course they don't. It's only a name. If it comes to that pigs don't have whistles!

PETER. Anyhow, Barbara—you see everything's all right——

(HICKETT *appears at back* C.)

BARBARA. Of course, I never wanted to doubt you, Peter, darling—only it was all so queer. And when I saw you from the train with Mrs. Hickett——

MARGUERITE. (*Crosses* R. *to* BARBARA.) Well, now you have seen me again I hope you realise there was nothing the matter.

(BONE *moves* R. *of table.*)

BARBARA. Yes, of course. Now that I know you stayed here with Mr. Hickett.

PETER. Yes. Hickett was here all right.

(BONE R. C. *sees* HICKETT *and makes violent gestures at* PETER. PETER *sees* BONE, *so does* BARBARA.)

What's up?

BARBARA. What's the matter? Mr. Hickett did stay here, didn't he?

PETER. Yes, yes.

MARGUERITE. Well, there is the book. You can see.

BARBARA. No, I don't want to see the book.

PETER. Oh, yes, you'd better see the book. Yes, you'd better see the book. (*Seeing* BONE *again, looks round and sees* HICKETT. *Gets confused and tries to change his plan of showing* BARBARA *the book.*) No, you'd better *not* see the book.

(HICKETT *crosses* D. L.)

(*To* BONE.) Nice fellow, Hickett, isn't he? You like him?

MAJOR BONE. Very.

PETER. You like him very. What about three half-hearted cheers for him?

PETER.
MAJOR BONE. } (*Together, weakly.*) Hooray, hooray, hooray!

BARBARA. All right, Peter, it's quite clear. He stayed here with you, and I quite believe it.

HICKETT. (*Coming down* L.) Then believe me, you're utterly wrong.

MAJOR BONE. Well meant, sir, but a bad spot. Do you mind not butting in?

MARGUERITE. (*Seeing* HICKETT.) Claude! You are being stupid and interfering!

BARBARA. Who are you, please?

HICKETT. I'm Mr. Hickett. Are you this man's wife?

BARBARA. Yes, of course I am.

HICKETT. I don't ask you to mistrust him. I don't mistrust my wife. But I think you'd better hear the truth.

BARBARA. Oh! (*Tiny pause. Turning to* PETER.) Then you haven't been telling me the truth?

PETER. The truth, what's that? I thought you would like to hear something else.

BARBARA. Peter! You've been lying to me!

PETER. Well, let me try again. I want to tell you the tale of the old copper pot.

MARGUERITE. I hope you don't think *I've* done anything wrong.

(BONE *makes his way behind table to* L. C,)

BARBARA. The best thing I can do is to see mother.

PETER. But Mrs. Hickett will tell you herself——

MARGUERITE. Of course I will.

BARBARA. I'd rather see mother.

(BONE *has moved* U. L. C.)

PETER. You'd rather see mother than Mrs. Hickett? You must be feverish.

(BARBARA *goes* U. L. C. *beside* BONE.)

MRS. BONE. (*Off.*) George!

(MRS. BONE *enters* R.)

George!

(BARBARA *comes down* L. C.)

Barbara—here you are! I should have been here to meet you. But, George—— (*To* BONE.) I've been chased by a bull! (*Falls on* BONE'S *shoulder.*)

(HICKETT *crosses behind* BARBARA *and goes over* R. *of* MARGUERITE.)

PETER. (*Takes* BARBARA'S *arm.*) I told you she'd been to see a cow and the bull didn't like it.

MRS. BONE. I suppose he's been trying to deceive you.

BARBARA. (*Crosses* L.) Mother, did Peter stay here last night?

MRS. BONE. Yes, he did. I came down with your father and found him in the same room as this woman.

PETER. (*To* MARGUERITE.) I wish that bull had caught her.

MRS. BONE. It's no use disguising. He's been false to you.

MARGUERITE. (*Indignantly. Crosses to* HICKETT C.) Now, do you think that can be true of *me*?

HICKETT. No. That I will not believe. (*Crosses up* R.)

(PETER *crosses* R.)

(MARGUERITE *turns up to* HICKETT *again. He remains half-hearted and uncertain.*)

MRS. BONE. George, call that chauffeur!

MAJOR BONE. (*Through bar door.*) Hi! you   Finish that up and come out of there! (*Crosses* L.)

MRS. BONE. (*To* BARBARA.) Come after us in *your* car to Bristol.

(*Enter* CHAUFFEUR *from bar, staggering.* MAJOR BONE *steadies him, gives him a gentle push, and he goes out through porch.*)

PETER. (*Crosses* D. L. *to* BARBARA.) Barbara, what are you going to do?

BARBARA. (*Crosses* D. L.) I'm going back to Bristol, after mother.

MRS. BONE. Yes. Immediately. (*Crosses up towards* C. *To* BONE.) George, are you coming?

MAJOR BONE. Is it optional?

MRS. BONE. No! Where's your hat?

MAJOR BONE. Here it is. (*Hat in bar. To* MRS. BONE.) You go ahead and get in the car.

MRS. BONE. Yes. I've something to say to you when we get in the car.

MAJOR BONE. Oh, then I'll ride on the top.

(*Exit* MRS. BONE *through porch, followed by* BONE.)

PETER. (*As* BARBARA *turns to follow.*) Barbara! Darling, listen to me!

(HICKETT, *who has been standing* R. *with* MARGUERITE, *who has given up trying to talk to him, now comes across and stops* BARBARA.)

BARBARA. No!

HICKETT. One moment!

(MARGUERITE *moves* L.)
(GLADYS *comes* D. R. C. *with dustpan.*)

MARGUERITE. There's Gladys. Ask her.

HICKETT. Did you see this lady and gentleman upstairs last night?

GLADYS. Yes, sur. I went into the room with Mrs. Spoker. She was in a rare temper with 'em.

HICKETT. Why was she?

GLADYS. (*Snorts.*) The lady were in bed. But Mrs. Spoker she couldn't get the gentleman to undress and go to bed too.

MARGUERITE. There you are !
PETER. Absolutely !
MARGUERITE. Just what I told you !
GLADYS. He kept pottering about and wouldn't settle.
PETER. That's right, Gladys. (*Crossing to her* R., *he shows her across* L.) What are you doing on Thursday ?

(*Exit* GLADYS.)

(*Car noises—hoots and back-fires.*)

(MAJOR *and* MRS. BONE *cross back of stage in taxi.*)

HICKETT. (*Crosses* L.) What is that ? .
PETER. It's the Bones rattling !
HICKETT. (*Crossing* R. *to* MARGUERITE.) I knew I could trust you.
MARGUERITE. Wait a moment, I want to hear what Mrs. Wykeham has got to say.
BARBARA. (*Crosses* C.) All I've got to say is that you missed the train on purpose, you brought her here, you stayed in her room, and you told lies—no, I'm going after mother.
HICKETT. I'm quite satisfied.
BARBARA. Then you are easily satisfied. (*To* PETER.) It's a preposterous story. (*Turns* U. C.)
PETER. Barbara, listen, please.
MARGUERITE. (*Crossing* R.) Oh, let her go. What does it matter ? The whole world will soon know now.
HICKETT. Marguerite——
MARGUERITE. Oh, Claude, I may have to hurt you—but I can't help it. (*Going to* PETER L.)

(HICKETT R.)

But when you love a man as I love Peter, what does anything matter ?

(BARBARA *comes down* R. C.)

I love you, Peter, and now that we missed that train and have taken the plunge, we will go out into the great world together and not worry what it thinks. Yes, yes, take me to Paris, Monte Carlo, Nice, up the Nile and down the Zambesi !

(BARBARA *comes down slowly.*)

PETER. Yes, we'll go to Hurst Park, Sandown and Goodwood.
MARGUERITE. Together, mine, mine ! (*Embraces* PETER.)
PETER. Yes, darling, let us go.
BARBARA. (*Crossing* L. *to* MARGUERITE.)   Leave my husband alone !
PETER. No ! (*Embracing* MARGUERITE.)
BARBARA. Oh ! Peter ! (*Sits on chair* L., *crying*.)
PETER. I can't keep it up, Barbara, darling. (*Crosses to her.*)
MARGUERITE. Don't worry, Claude, you haven't lost me yet. (*Crossing* R.)
    (*Enter* MRS. SPOKER.)
HICKETT. I never doubted you.
PETER. I never doubted you. I was only teasing.
MARGUERITE. Sweetheart !
PETER. Darling !
MRS. SPOKER. What is this I hear ?
PETER. (*To* MRS. SPOKER, *unconsciously.*) It's nothing—darling—— (*Looks into* MRS. SPOKER'S *face.*) Oh ! (*Then kneels at* BARBARA'S *side.*)

MRS. SPOKER

HICKETT   MARGUERITE   BARBARA
                                 PETER

CURTAIN

Lightning Source UK Ltd.
Milton Keynes UK
UKOW06f0013120816

280504UK00001B/9/P